Addressing Learning Differences

Sensory Integration

Practical Strategies and Sensory Motor Activities for Use in the Classroom

by Michael C. Abraham, C.A.P.E.

Cover Design
by Terri Moll

Inside Illustrations
by Darcy Bell-Myers

LDA
An imprint of Carson-Dellosa Publishing LLC
Greensboro, North Carolina

Author: Michael C. Abraham, C.A.P.E.
Editors: Debra Olson Pressnall, Kathryn Wheeler
Interior Artist: Darcy Bell-Myers
Photo Credits: © EyeWire

LDA
An imprint of Carson-Dellosa Publishing LLC
PO Box 35665
Greensboro, NC 27425 USA

ISBN 978-0-74240-268-3
165108091

Preface

People are constantly bombarded with sensory information through their experiences of the environment and by contact with others. For most children, sensory integration develops naturally and even unremarkably in early play activities. Adapting to new sensations becomes ordinary as play progresses. When children enter a classroom, they are bombarded by sensory stimuli that they need to process. The ongoing and natural flow of classroom activities, varied teacher styles, and the curriculum provide a mix of information that children must regulate through their central nervous systems. These sensory stimuli are the building blocks with which children organize, understand, and maneuver through their environment. Usually, the ability to process sensory information is easy, automatic, and effortless.

Decoding and regulating sensory information, however, can be challenging and overwhelming for children with sensory integration (SI) dysfunction. Children with SI dysfunction have a hard time knowing which sensory information is important and which is irrelevant. For them, adaptation does not take place naturally. They register sensations inconsistently, day in and day out. Some days they appear to be focused, but on others they are not even aware of the task. These children simply do not have the efficient kind of brain functions that enable most people to be consistent from one day to another. When this occurs, learning is affected in cognitive, motor, and emotional development. Specific exercises can be offered to lessen the dysfunction. By providing classroom teachers with instructional techniques that target sensory-motor skills, educators can effectively enhance the ability of sensory-challenged learners to take in and regulate sensory information.

Table of Contents

0-7424-0268-1 • Sensory Integration

Introduction

Our educational systems are changing to meet the needs of children. Educators must revise curricula as they try to forecast the future educational needs of all their students. The pace of instruction, classroom size, curricula, and teaching styles are only a few of the current influences on how children learn. Including SI-challenged children in the regular classroom can seem a formidable assignment. This book is written to provide teachers with specific examples of how to rise to the task.

Federal law ensures that students with special needs get an equal and appropriate education within the public school system. Special needs include the following conditions:
► Attention deficit disorder (ADD)
► Autism
► Deafness
► Deaf-blindness
► Hearing impairment
► Mental retardation
► Neurological impairment
► Orthopedic impairment
► Serious emotional disturbance
► Specific learning disability
► Traumatic brain injury (TBI)
► Visual handicap

When students with SI dysfunction participate in the ordinary classroom, they can at times be overwhelmed by the sensory stimulation around them. Sound educational practices will help these children complete specific tasks successfully in the classroom atmosphere. The teacher's challenge is to discover their learning styles and offer interventions to assist them. The activities in this book are provided to help children learn how their bodies work as they negotiate the environment and incoming stimuli. Through constant repetition and continuity of experience, children can learn to regulate their vestibular, tactile, visual, auditory, and proprioceptive (kinesthetic) awareness. This will let the children be in tune with their bodies and how they function.

What Is Sensory Integration?

The central nervous system develops after birth in response to incoming stimulation through the five senses. For example, the sense of space—the knowledge of where the limbs and trunk are and what they are doing—is critical to any developing child. For children with SI problems, this sense may not be intact. They have an irregularity in brain function. In the realm of tactile sense, for example, input from the touch of other people and objects of all kinds may not be processed or modulated correctly through the central nervous system. These children seem unable to organize tactile sensations, let alone coordinate them with vision and hearing.

The term *sensory integration dysfunction* is used to characterize this disability. Sensory integration dysfunction may present itself in cognitive, motor, social/emotional, speech/language, or attention disorders. When children have sensory integration (SI) dysfunction, they may be unable to respond to sensory information or to plan and organize accurately what they need to do in school or at home.

Some signs of SI dysfunction are:
► Delays in academic achievement
► Delays in speech, language, or motor skills
► Difficulty making transitions from one situation to another
► High degree of distractibility
► Impulsivity
► Inability to unwind or calm self
► Over- or under-sensitivity to touch, movement, sights, or sounds
► Physical clumsiness
► Poor self-concept or self-esteem
► Social and/or emotional problems
► Unusually high or unusually low activity level

Important Sensory—Motor Integration Skills

Input from our senses is part of all movement experiences. The following skills are used each time a person engages in fine or gross motor movements. For children with SI dysfunction, special programs can be planned to assist in the development of certain skills by offering exercises that target specific needs.

Equilibrium

Equilibrium refers to body movements or shifts to maintain or regain balance. The movement can be small, such as maintaining a sitting position in a car that is turning a corner, or large, such as protecting the body from a fall by using one's arms and hands. Activities for improving equilibrium must be developmentally appropriate for the child with special needs.

Kinesthetic

Kinesthesia or proprioception pertains to information from inside the body—especially from muscles, joints, and ligaments—about the body's condition and position in space. It is the internal awareness about our body parts that allows us to perform tasks with coordination. Co-contraction involves activity of muscles on both sides of a joint contracting together. Co-contraction is a type of joint stability and is very important for coordinated movement.

Motor Planning

Motor planning refers to a person's ability to organize, plan, and then execute new or unpracticed motor tasks. The sensory systems, especially tactile, are of prime importance for motor planning.

Tactile

Tactile refers to the sensory messages received through our skin. Tactile information is a basis for learning about external objects as well as the condition of our body. If this information is not precise, it can hinder learning and coordination.

Vestibular

The vestibular mechanism is located in the inner ear and is activated by movement or by changing one's head position. The vestibular system, in coordination with the kinesthetic and visual systems, directs the central nervous system to the position in space and to the force of gravity so the child can maintain equilibrium. Maintaining equilibrium is a result of a functioning vestibular system. Practice in this area promotes more efficient movement, balance, equilibrium, and vestibular processing and integration. Activities should be encouraged but not forced on a child.

Bilateral Motor Coordination

Bilateral motor coordination is the ability to coordinate both sides of one's body. Movements can be either reciprocal or bilateral. Bilateral motor coordination can be achieved when tactile and kinesthetic information is processed.

How It Feels to Lack Sensory Integration

Unreliable Sensations

Unable to organize sensations into coherent information, children with SI dysfunction often do not develop normal perceptions. Yet these are needed to understand school work and situations. Imagine trying to learn when sensations feel like an endless series of magician's tricks.

When poor sensory processing exists, children pay little attention or may overreact to a given task. They have little or no interest in doing things that are purposeful or constructive. Often these children are in motion, indicating a potential Attention Deficit Disorder (ADD) or Attention Deficit Hyperactivity Disorder (ADHD). They may not modulate input well, especially vestibular information (the brain's understanding of balance and equilibrium as the child negotiates the environment and tactile sensations). The children may be gravitationally insecure or defensive about touch. They may be moving constantly to find the center of gravity or a comfort level as they sit in a chair or on the floor, or when they try to stand. They may crave or need to spin. These children may alternately avoid or covet touch, which in turn will place them in a state of movement.

Auditory and Visual Input Compromised

Part of the brain in the limbic system (which decides which sensory input is to be registered and brought to our attention) also decides whether a person will do something about that information. Research shows that this part may not be working well in the brains of children with sensory integration dysfunction. They do not register observations that everyone else notices. More often than with other sensory inputs, auditory and visual inputs are ignored or not registered. Sometimes the children may over-register one sound and under-register another. Their visual environment can be compromised, too. They may stare through people or avoid looking them in the eyes. They often pay no attention to objects and playthings. However, sometimes their brains will decide to give the most careful and prolonged attention to tiny details, such as lines on the floor. (Once again, this may appear as an ADD issue.)

Confused Priorities

An ordinary classroom is rife with stimulation. Children with SI dysfunction have difficulty decoding and knowing which visual information is important at the moment and which is insignificant. They will often have trouble registering other sensations as well, such as a light touch or deep pressure. The child may show no reaction or may respond negatively to another person's touch. Often these children will not acknowledge levels of pain when experiencing a fall or a bump unless it is very intense. Some children are overly sensitive to the texture of things. Young toddlers and preschoolers may resist solid food because they do not like its feel. There may also be problems with smell and taste. Children with sensory problems may not be able to register odors; conversely, they may overreact to certain odors. They may lack a sense of taste.

Sensory input through muscles and joints may be greater for these children than through their eyes and ears. Pulling and pushing their arms and legs at the joints appears to feel satisfying. This important proprioceptive information helps to ground the children and gives them a feeling of security as the strong sensations are registered in their brains. These children may seek movement and vestibular stimulation strenuously or reject it entirely. Neither response is normal.

Ineffective Modulation

Modulation is the brain's regulation of its own activity and involves helping some neural messages to produce more of a response, inhibiting other messages to reduce extraneous activity (overflow). In some children, their brains fail to vary the intensity of vestibular sensations (e.g., spinning, jumping, swinging) and touch. In turn, these children can resist movement and become insecure because they cannot control the sensation. (For example, they may not feel grounded when they are in the lap of an adult while they are swinging). They can become extremely anxious about their relationship to gravity and space. If children are gravitationally insecure, they are at least registering a sensation. Since the children may not be proficient in registering many of the sensations from the environment, they cannot harmonize these sensations to form a clear perception of and relationship to a place. They may take a long time to process information visually. Even when they see something, children with SI dysfunction may not comprehend it adequately. When new experiences are presented, they may react with alarm and resistance. Therapy can improve these reactions. Only after many repeated similar experiences

will the children recognize certain places or events as familiar and safe. Some children may have so much trouble registering the spatial elements of their environments that they can be upset whenever anything is changed in a room at home or at school.

Difficulty in Planning Movements

Without normal registration of sensory information from the skin, muscles, joints, and vestibular system, children with dysfunction cannot develop a good, clear perception of the body. They may lack good neuronal models (a good understanding of their body parts, body part functions, and how they move within the environment), both of themselves and of the world. Good motor planning is a product of a well-modulated central nervous system. Poor sensory processing hinders the motor-planning capacity from many angles:

- The child cannot readily understand the object in front of her.
- She does not have well-developed body perception to use for motor planning.
- She has trouble abstracting the potential use of an object.
- The child is reluctant to engage in purposeful activity.
- She resists doing anything new and different.
- When the child does something, it may not deliver the intended pleasurable experience.

Normal human behavior organizes perception and responds to observations. Children who cannot perceive their physical environment well or act effectively upon that environment lack the basic material for organizing more complex behaviors. If they cannot organize simple adaptive motor responses, such as sitting with upright posture or moving from sitting to standing position, the children will have trouble with more complex behaviors, such as movements through environments that require processing of vestibular, tactile, and proprioceptive information.

The Objective of Intervention

The teacher's or parent's goal:

▶ To improve sensory processing so that more sensations will be effectively registered and modulated

▶ To encourage children to form simple adaptive responses that will help them to organize behavior and learning

Ideas and Principles of Intervention for the Student Included in the Classroom

The primary goal of intervention is to enable SI-challenged children to form a sense of their personhood. As this sense of self develops, earlier and more fundamental levels of motor milestones serve as a foundation for newer levels of adaptive responses to sensory information. Intervention should not simply engage the children's language, motor functioning, or cognition skills. Working with any of these domains in isolation may just continue a sense of fragmentation.

Intervention must strive to foster three things: 1) focus and concentration, 2) engagement with the human world, and 3) two-way intentional communication. These activities will promote interactive experiences children can use to abstract a sense of who they are. Teachers and parents must pay attention to the children's regulatory difficulties. That is, how does each the child best learn in the realms of visual, auditory, tactile, and vestibular stimuli? Is a child reactive or underactive to these stimuli? Follow each child's interests and provide opportunities that allow the child to experience a visceral sense of pleasure and intimacy. This leads the child to want to focus upon the present task.

Gestural Interaction

Opening and closing circles of communication is the primary unit of gestural interaction and it creates a foundation for all subsequent communication. Children need forms of communication in which they can have an opportunity to process information receptively and, in turn, to express themselves. For those children who have very little or no verbal communication skills, gestural interaction is important. Using sign language, gestural language, and picture boards, a circle of communication is formed; the child can then receive and express language. If a child has a great need to move and/or a short attention span, a teacher can use this need to motivate the child to create a circle of communication. A perceptive teacher can use a picture board or any other device used for communication with the child to encourage him or her to explain what is needed (in this case to get up and move). By stopping the present activity and fulfilling the child's wishes (swinging in a net swing, going out to the playground, etc.), a complete circle of communication is made, providing a foundation for future levels of two-way communication.

Relating to children when they are experiencing strong feelings is critical. When they are motivated, for example, to negotiate to get a certain kind of food or to go outside, there is often an opportunity to open and close many circles. Be sure to stretch these transition times and the periods of negotiation, because children can only learn to think abstractly and generalize through active experiences. Most children seek activities that provide beneficial sensory experiences during their development. It is this active involvement and exploration that enables them to become more mature, efficient organizers of sensory information.

Scheduling Movement Activities

Movement experiences should be not be scheduled and then neglected. Rather, they should be more spontaneous and integrated within the school day. Children with SI dysfunction require far more practice in some areas of skill development. They need play and movement to lay the foundation for developing habits that affect their ability to read, write, and think. Without early opportunities to engage in learning through action, many young children begin school with inadequate motor skill development. Children with SI dysfunction will not go on to acquire these motor skills through "natural" experiences later on in life.

Movement—Building Strengths for the Future

Minimize Learning Disabilities

Providing early opportunities for movement may help minimize or eliminate potential types of learning disabilities. Perceptual problems do not become identified as such until the demands of second grade. Readiness skills, including writing and cutting which require the child to understand the right and left sides of the body (laterality), are usually attained by the second-grade level. The child can and should be able to use the right and left sides as in stabilizing the paper with one hand as the other writes, or in holding the paper in one hand as the other cuts. The movement activities which seem to relate most directly are those which incorporate movement on opposite sides of the body, such as crawling, hand-over-hand climbing, and moving on a balance beam.

Children with special needs who have many opportunities to develop their shoulders and upper-arm muscles will have better fine-motor control for handwriting. Because we develop from head to toe and from our trunk out to our hands, we need to work with strengthening the upper arms and shoulders before expecting the hands and fingers to be well coordinated. Climbing on jungle gyms, wheel-barrel walking, crawling through tunnels and under obstacles, working at the easel, and making exaggerated arm movements during fingerplays and songs all help develop the muscles needed for writing.

Work from Concrete to Abstract

Children learn from concrete to abstract, and their bodies provide the most concrete experience available for planning and organizational skills. Children must first experience controlling their bodies in space before they can organize pictures and letters on a page. Also, children who have many opportunities to use their bodies in a predetermined sequence (as in an obstacle course or a movement song) are learning the abstract sequencing skills of beginning, middle, and end—how to order and plan, anticipate the next segment, and experience closure. These important skills are also required on the abstract level for reading comprehension and creative thinking.

Stimulate the Brain

When children move their bodies, they are concurrently stimulating the corresponding areas of the brain that relate to abstract thinking. Although this is a tremendous oversimplification, it is a well-accepted fact that movement on the right side of the body stimulates the left side of the brain, which, in turn, controls systematic, convergent thinking. Conversely, movement on the left side of the body stimulates the right side of the brain, which is associated with creative, divergent thinking. When both sides of the body are involved, it physiologically stimulates the connections between the two sides of the brain and literally helps the child develop more cohesive and extensive thinking skills. This includes all activities such as: crossing midline ("Simon says, touch your right ear with your left hand"), balancing, crawling, jumping, running, swinging, and using large manipulatives or materials requiring two hands.

Improve Social Development

Movement has direct impact on the social/emotional development of young children. Discipline problems are often related to restricted or inadequate movement opportunities. Children who need to run, jump, and climb will find inappropriate uses for their energy if the classroom does not provide enough constructive outlets. For many children, one short period of outside play is not adequate. They need access to a variety of movement activities throughout the day.

The Benefits of Play

Society tends to underrate the importance of play. Since most children play adequately without parental help, and since it is not easy to see how the brain develops, most adults think play is mere entertainment or fooling around. However, children's play before they go to school is just as important for their development as is their schoolwork.

Play is essential for developing the capacity to plan motor movements. As they play, children move their body parts in countless different ways, and the sensations from these movements add new sensory maps to their bodily perceptions. Through large, full-body movements, they learn how to relate themselves to the space around them. Through manipulation of small play objects, they learn to use their hands and fingers efficiently. Play expands competence.

If a child does not play with as many different playthings as other children, parents tend to think that she is just not interested in that type of play. However, the child who is not interested in the normal range of play probably has a problem, and that problem usually includes a sensory processing disorder. The dyspraxic child's play is very limited, because she has trouble with motor planning and so must stick to simple and familiar games. The child with a vestibular problem is restricted by poor postural responses or by the anxiety caused by vestibular input that she cannot modulate. Simply, the vestibular system is responsible for balance and equilibrium. If processed correctly, vestibular input tells the child where he is in relationship to others and objects in the environment. A child may possess a processing problem with vestibular input due to symptoms of hypervestibular or hypovestibular problems. Teacher and parents can observe symptoms the child may exhibit.

Vestibular Problems

Hypervestibular problems surface when a child cannot modulate the amount of sensory information attaching the central nervous system. The child who is hypervestibular may demonstrate some of the following symptoms:

- Cannot inhibit vestibular information entering the central nervous system
- Dislikes seeing or doing spinning activities
- Experiences dizziness going down slides, riding in a car, or jumping
- Avoids the playground and sports (such as gymnastics) that provide too much stimulation
- May feel as if he is constantly in motion and losing balance
- May get dizzy or nauseous when riding on buses, trains, or subways
- Prefers to ride in front seat of cars
- Feels dizzy on escalators, elevators, and entrances to and from escalators
- Avoids relatives and adults who toss him in the air
- Usually uncoordinated; avoids sports and other gross motor activities
- Retreats to books and usually completes academic work successfully

Hypovestibular problems surface when a child cannot process proprioceptive information as it impacts movement, force, and direction. The child does not receive the needed vestibular stimulation to react to the force of gravity, or to his or her position in space as it relates to others and objects in the environment. The child who is hypovestibular may demonstrate some of the following symptoms:

► Has low muscle tone which causes poor body awareness
► Experiences poor balance and frequent falls
► Has clumsy and uncoordinated movement patterns; usually not successful in sports
► Has poor static muscle control; unable to sit or stand still for academics or activities
► Has trouble knowing position in space (standing, sitting, falling, etc.)
► Craves doing or watching spinning activities
► Never gets dizzy when spinning
► Has laterality problems—knowing and using body parts in a coordinated way
► Often has delay in language, reading, and writing
► Trouble moving arms and legs against an unstable trunk (the whole body moves)
► Lacks ability to control eye muscles, which interferes with academics and movement
► May avoid playing with other children because she does not like to be touched or to touch others

Self-Fulfillment and Competence

The essential ingredient in children's play is expression of their inner drive toward self-fulfillment as a sensory-motor creature. Children need to follow their inner drive toward physical activity in which they master their environment and own bodies. Physical activity produces sensory stimulation and adaptive responses that help to organize the brain.

Through play, children obtain the sensory input from their bodies and from gravity that is essential for both motor and emotional (sense of oneself) development. The sensations are what make it fun. All locomotor activities produce a tremendous amount of vestibular, proprioceptive, and tactile input to the brain. Children play to capture this input. The more they explore, the more their senses are stimulated, and the more complex is the adaptive response required.

Strategies and Techniques

Here are the basic principles that teachers and parents can follow when they help children with this dysfunction:

► Treat all children with dignity and respect.
► Establish rapport and be trustworthy.
► Build learning through repetition and continuity.
► Always use direct eye-to-eye contact.
► Build on the children's strengths, not their weaknesses.

Preparing the Environment

► Prepare the environment with as little sensory stimulation as possible. Reduce the number of papers on the walls. Reduce/ eliminate hanging projects. Reduce the noise level. Be aware of fluorescent lighting and sunlight through the windows, etc.

► Avoid "highs" within the classroom atmosphere. Rather, be a calming force and strive to maintain a calm atmosphere.

► Increase attention spans by removing distracting objects (such as toys, games, projects, and pets—all within the visual field of the child.)

► Equipment (scissors, paintbrushes, etc.) should not be presented until the children are ready to use them. The child will be distracted by the object and will not be listening carefully to your directions.

► Encourage children to help put the equipment away after the activity period in order to connect with the group and develop responsible behaviors.

Developing Class Atmosphere

► Provide your students an opportunity to develop their body images through movement that uses rhythms, music, and other sensory-motor activities.

► Use short, direct, and simple instructions.

► Set up the class with routines and orderly procedures. When students know what is coming next, they feel more secure.

► Make children secure by using experiences that are not threatening and are developmentally appropriate.

► Do not strive for control at all times. Allow free play periods and intermittent breaks.

► Always be consistent in dealing with behaviors within the classroom.

► Other teachers (occupational therapist, physical therapists, speech pathologist, PE instructor, etc.) should have the same plan when dealing with behavioral issues.

► The program should be student-orientated, not curriculum based!

► Employ short periods of intense movement and alternate with quiet activities.

► Teachers need to find out from parents what motivates each child the most.

Presenting Class Activities

► Offer positive experiences at the present level of functioning of the children.

► Force nothing upon the children.

► There is never a right or wrong expectation, but rather an experiential encounter with the curriculum.

► Provide instructions one-to-one and in a small group.

► Take individual needs into account when planning an activity.

► Move to music. Simple, repetitive patterns provide a calming atmosphere for children.

► Provide a variety of activities so all children will have a chance with success.

► Structure activities so that the children move and engage in developing physical fitness.

► Change directions and movement patterns to increase body awareness.

► When reaction time for processing incoming stimuli is slow, permit the following clues separately. First, allow the child to use visual cues. Next, use auditory cues. Third, provide tactile cues.

► Use music to signal closure for children. They will begin to understand a beginning and ending to the activity through music.

► All activities should be short to accommodate brief attention spans. Each child is unique. Gradually increase the length of the activity based on the child's needs.

► Repetition of skills allows the child to explore the possibilities of engaging in an activity appropriately and/or successfully.

► Children progress at their own rate, not ours.

Dealing with Behaviors

► When preservative behaviors exist (e.g., rocking back and forth, preservation on an idea or action), understand that these acts constitute the sum of the children's sensory experiences. This may be their maximum ability for dealing with reality. Teachers must understand and intervene in an appropriate manner.

► Provide immediate, positive reinforcement for desired behavior.

► Observe facial expressions and body gestures. Anticipate future behaviors of the children.

► Discourage preservative behaviors that can develop into rigid behavioral patterns. Know the child; know when to intervene.

Increasing Social Interaction

► Develop communication skills with short, small steps so children will increase their awareness of others. This will lay a foundation for helping young children learn how to relate to others.

► Partner and group participation are desirable because of the social contacts children make necessary. A gradual process of working with partners should take place.

What Parents Can Do

More than anyone else, parents make a world of difference in helping their children who have learning or behavior problems to develop better sensory integration.

Three Different Types of Parental Involvement

Parents can be highly involved in their child's life and education. They may be dominant and knowledgeable about their child and are in constant contact with the schools to make sure the program is responsive.

Parents can be supportive and reliable, asking questions and supporting the program because they feel it is appropriate. They follow through at home if asked to do so.

Parents can be passive because they feel unable to deal with their child's problems or simply may not know how to get more involved.

Important Steps to Take

► **Recognize and understand the problem so that you can take action on what your child needs.**

It is easy to recognize unpleasant behavior but more difficult to comprehend the nervous system disorder that underlies that behavior. When a child behaves poorly, it is important to realize that most of that troublesome behavior may come from sensations that the child cannot integrate. If the child cannot organize sensations, he cannot organize behavior.

A delay in speech development is another clue to sensory integration dysfunction. Speech depends upon many sensory-motor functions, and so it is often delayed whenever any part of the brain does not work efficiently.

It is true that children do develop at different rates, but one of the biggest mistakes a parent can make is to think that the child with this dysfunction will outgrow the problem. If therapy and intervention through the schools are to be effective, the brain must be young and flexible. Start early!

► **Help your child to feel all right about herself. Control the child's environment to prevent over-stimulation.**

Early recognition will certainly help the whole family see the child's behavior in the proper perspective, so that they can give the child extra acceptance, consideration, and structure. They can provide activities and family fun that the child can handle. (See the continued discussion Three Things that Contribute to a Negative Self-Image.)

► **Help the child learn how to play.**

Another mistake is to think that an intellectual approach alone will help the child, as though she could be trained to do things the brain is not able to do. A sensory-motor approach is more helpful to a young child. Start playing together.

► **Work together with the schools and outside professionals.**

One of the common errors made by professionals today is to assume that behavior problems can be corrected without doing something to change the brain dysfunction producing those behaviors. A perceived inappropriate behavior of "hitting" can be determined by a teacher or parent as "bad behavior." There may be numerous reasons for displaying this behavior; however, some children who do not have their tactile systems intact react negatively (hitting others, shoving, pushing, etc.) when another child approaches their personal space or touches them. The sensory information of touch may not be regulated appropriately (light touch or deep pressure) and in turn the child can respond with a "flight or fight" response. Thus, the "hitting behavior" is a product of a sensory disorder within the tactile system. This child should not be labeled as a "bad child." Various activities can be provided for tactile or touching activities. Many arts and crafts activities offer numerous textures for tactile input. Activities with shaving cream, soap, crayons, play clay, or food preparation can be fun tactile additions to a day. A sandbox can be a valuable tool for exploration. Provide contents that are varied and easily graded (such as styrene foam packing pieces, dried beans, rice, leaves, sand, and walnuts).

Accentuate the Positive

Three Things That Contribute to a Negative Self-Image . . .
- The way the nervous system is functioning.
- The feelings of frustration and inadequacy that arise when the child cannot do things well.
- Other people's negative reactions to what the child does.

Ways to Build Self-Image

Parents need to realize that the child's problem is a physical one. It involves the action of electrical impulses and chemicals in the brain. A learning disorder or behavior problem resulting from brain dysfunction is just as much a physical problem as a broken leg or the measles.

The child's nervous system is not as stable as other children's. Too much stimulation in the form of movement, people, changes in schedule, noise, demands, or illness can cause the child to lose control of emotions. This can be especially true if the child is tactilely defensive or gravitationally insecure.

If the child loses his temper or self-control, punishment will only lower self-concept further. Instead of punishment, the child needs something that will help him regain composure. A quiet place, such as the child's own room, away from the stress of incoming stimuli, will aid more than anything else will. When the brain becomes disorganized, do not think "punishment." Instead, control the amount of the sensory input from the environment to help the child's brain reorganize.

Discipline is still necessary for family sanity. Rewarding good behavior and taking away privileges for inappropriate behavior is a basic principle of discipline.

Parents sometimes damage their child's self-concept by having expectations that are too high for him to fulfill. Because we cannot see a sensory integrative dysfunction, it is easy to forget that the child has a disability and cannot do as well as other children. Structure in the environment helps the unstable brain preserve its stability. Good organization in the child's home life will promote good organization of the brain.

Organization centers on time and place. The environment that touches the child's skin can have the greatest effect, negative or positive, on his nervous system. Respect your child's response to sensory stimuli. In addition, certain odors and tastes can be quite offensive to the child. The most important thing is to realize that the child simply perceives things differently.

Children's responses to vestibular information may be just as varied as their responses to tactile input. Some love it; some do not. Merely rocking in a rocking chair may be as much as one particular child can tolerate. Others seek a lot of vestibular stimulation. Give the child an environment in which she can move! The child's relationship to gravity is critical. This includes the ability to possess appropriate muscle tone and strength. The child needs to be comfortable with gravity in order to have normal activities in the future.

Children need proper muscle tone and strength to control posture. The vestibular system controls these factors. When children need to sit at their desks, we take for granted that they have the muscle strength and control to sit for periods of time and complete work. However, some children are constantly moving in their chairs and often will stand next to their desks, walk around the room, or kneel on their chairs to work. They are fighting the force of gravity and do not possess the necessary strength or postural control to sit for long periods of time. Teachers will often interpret this movement as hyperactive but in reality it may be a problem with the vestibular system and the hypotonus.

Developmental Milestones

Understanding the developmental milestones for children as they grow is important so that teachers can plan appropriate movement activities and interventions for children with SI dysfunction. The list below provides a guide to normal development of motor skills. These developmental milestones should be used only as guidelines. Acquisition of these milestones can take place six to eight months on either side of the listed ages. Children with special needs may not meet these developmental milestones at their chronological ages. Therefore, this information allows teachers to adjust their expectations before an activity is selected. Teachers must know as much as they can about the motor levels of their students before the activity takes place.

Average Age at Which a Child May Reach These Milestones

1 MONTH
- On back, head usually to one side
- On tummy, turns head when put down
- Looks at mobiles and faces
- Cuddles during feeding

2 MONTHS
- On back, turns head side-to-side
- On tummy, lifts head momentarily
- Eyes follow moving persons and objects
- Smiles responsively; coos

3 MONTHS
- On back, head more centered
- On tummy, lifts head 2-3 inches (5-8 cm) off crib surface
- Hands open most of the time
- Looks at hands
- Eyes focus on stationary objects
- Chuckles

4 MONTHS
- On back, head centered and hands together on chest
- On tummy, head up and looking forward
- Plays with own fingers; grasps rattle
- Pulls clothes off face
- Babbles; smiles and vocalizes at mirror
- Rolls to side from back
- Performs ulnar palmer grasp—ring finger and little finger against palm

5 MONTHS
- On back, lifts legs and sees feet
- Brings hands together for toys
- Rolls back to tummy; on tummy, gets up on hands
- Takes weight on feet in standing
- Looks after dropped toy
- Laughs and squeals
- Discriminates strangers
- Performs palmer grasp—"gross grasp"—grasps objects against palm, not using thumb
- Rolls side to side from supine position

6 MONTHS
- Holds foot while lying on back
- Rolls from tummy to back position
- Sits with propping
- Shakes rattle; reaches for toy
- Pats self in mirror
- Tries out new sounds
- Protective extension-forward reactions
- Holds head erect in sitting position with support

7 MONTHS
- Puts feet in mouth
- Crawls on tummy; pivots in a circle on tummy
- Sits for a short time
- Mouths toys
- Bangs toys
- Transfers toys from hand to hand
- Imitates sounds
- Sits independently but may use hands

8 MONTHS
- Sits for a long time
- Stands holding on
- Holds two toys; drops toy on purpose
- Plays peekaboo
- Feeds self cracker; drinks liquid from cup
- Responds to name
- Protective extension back reactions
- Rolls from back to tummy position

9 MONTHS
- Creeps on hands and knees
- Goes from sitting to tummy and tummy to sitting
- Bounces up and down while in a standing position
- Pokes at things with index finger
- Picks up small ball
- Plays patty-cake; waves bye-bye
- Performs radial digital grasp; uses thumb, index, and middle finger, not palm
- Stands holding on

10 MONTHS
- Pulls up to stand in crib
- Gets down from standing
- Says "da da" and "ma ma"
- Understands "no"
- Hugs and loves toy
- Offers toy to others
- Pushes arm through during dressing
- Uses inferior pincer grasp—index, thumb using lower part of index finger
- Crawls on fours (reciprocally)

11 MONTHS
- Cruises along furniture for balance
- Walks with two hands held
- Pivots in sitting position
- Picks up small block; gives toy when asked
- Lifts blanket to find toy
- Says two to three "words"
- Lifts feet during dressing
- Drinks from cup
- Reaches sitting position by self

12 MONTHS
- Stands alone momentarily
- Squats to play
- Makes steps from one object to another
- Picks up small cracker
- Grasps crayon in fist and imitates scribbling
- Says four to six "words"
- Pats pictures in books; communicates by pointing
- Plays ball with others
- Creeping-plantigrade on hands and feet
- Hopping reaction; stagger reactions
- Rolls ball forward from a sitting position
- Assumes and maintains kneeling
- Walks with one hand held
- Uses neat pincer grasp—uses precise thumb and finger opposition
- Crawls with coordination

15 MONTHS
- Walks alone and seldom falls; runs stiffly
- Squats to play; stands up from squat
- Walks up stairs with one hand held
- Climbs on chair to reach things
- Hurls ball
- Scribbles spontaneously
- Has a 10-20 word vocabulary
- Points to one body part
- Feeds with spoon, but spills
- Plays with pull toys
- Can point to two of own body parts

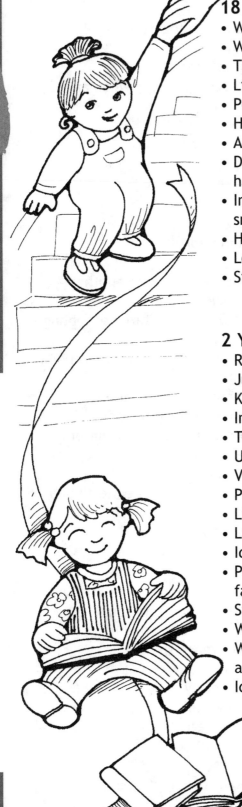

18 MONTHS

- Walks down stairs with one hand held
- Walks into large ball to kick; tries to jump
- Turns two to four pages together
- Likes to stack a few blocks
- Points to own nose, eyes, hair, and mouth
- Has a 20-30 word vocabulary
- Asks for "more" and "drink"
- Drinks well from cup and uses spoon; puts on hat; takes off socks
- Imitates Mom and Dad in play; seats self in small chair
- Hurls ball from standing position without falling
- Log rolls
- Stands on one foot with help

2 YEARS

- Runs well
- Jumps down from bottom step
- Kicks large ball; throws ball forward
- Imitates vertical stroke and circular scribble
- Turns book pages one at a time
- Unscrews some parts of toys
- Vocabulary has too many words to count
- Points to body parts; names at least one
- Likes pretend play; feeds doll
- Likes to help around house
- Identifies self in mirror
- Performs palmer supinate grasp; turns palm facing up
- Stoops and recovers
- Walks backward
- Walks upstairs and downstairs alone without alternating feet, holding onto the rail
- Identifies two body parts from a picture

2 1/2 YEARS
- Jumps with both feet off floor
- Tries to stand on one foot with help
- Alternates feet going up stairs
- Imitates horizontal stroke; imitates circle
- Pours liquid from glass to glass
- Names seven body parts
- Expresses self in three to four word sentences
- Answers simple questions; e.g., "What does a doggie say?"
- Knows "big" and "little"
- Pulls up pants; finds armholes correctly
- Puts shoes on, any foot

3 YEARS
- Rides tricycle using pedals
- Alternates feet while going down stairs
- Stands on one foot 2–3 seconds
- Walks on tiptoes
- Throws overhand
- Holds crayons by fingers
- Copies circle, vertical, and horizontal lines
- Tries to cut with scissors
- Knows "up/down" and "loud/soft"
- Matches colors and identifies two colors
- Likes to play with other children
- Understands turn-taking; likes to make-believe
- Washes and dries hands
- Uses digital pronate (palm downward) grasp
- Jumps on both feet
- Jumps from 12" height—one foot leading

3 1/2 YEARS
- Builds tower of nine to ten 1" cubes
- Catches bounced ball
- Folds a sheet of paper
- Draws any two parts of a six-part stick figure
- Identifies six to ten body parts
- Stands on tiptoes for 10 seconds
- Stands on one foot alone for 1-2 seconds

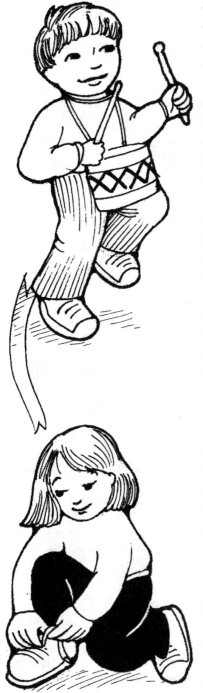

4 YEARS
- Marches rhythmically to music
- Hops on one foot; tries to skip
- Positions arms to catch ball
- Tries to cut on line; likes to paint
- Uses words like "pretty," "big," "happy" appropriately
- Counts to five; uses eight- to nine-word sentences
- Repeats all of a nursery rhyme or song
- Dresses self except for tying bows
- Puts shoes on correct feet
- Likes to make things from clay or blocks
- Plays with children in a group
- Pumps self on swing
- Runs smoothly at different speeds
- Bounces ball and catches it; catches object tossed from other
- Static tripod posture
- Stands on one foot alone for 3–8 seconds
- Hops on one foot
- Runs smoothly at different speeds
- Draws any four parts of a six-part stick figure (4.5 years)

5 YEARS
- Gallops in order to skip; plays on monkey bars
- Tries to turn somersaults
- Rides bicycle with training wheels
- Catches large ball with two hands
- Copies square and triangle shapes
- Likes cutting, pasting, and coloring
- Draws picture of a person with body
- Names five colors; prints name
- Knows 1+1=2, 1+2=3; counts to 10
- Likes puzzles and shape-matching
- Ties shoes
- Likes school
- Throws ball up and catches it; throws with some control
- Dynamic tripod posture—The ability of the child to hold the writing implement with

a pincer grasp (thumb, index finger, and middle finger) and negotiate the writing process

5 1/2 YEARS
- Prone extension (Superman) 10 seconds
- Flexor supine (butt) 10 seconds
- Walks on 1" (25mm) line for 12' (3.66 m), heel to toe
- Dribbles large ball with one hand (8")
- Strikes ball with bat on string
- Crumples a piece of paper into a ball
- Points front, back, near, up, down, with eyes closed
- Knows some body-part functions
- Knows all body parts

6 YEARS
- Skips
- Walks on 1" (25 mm) wide line for at least 12' (3.66 m)
- Dribbles ball with one hand with control
- Strikes ball on string with bat
- Advanced throwing—the ability to step in opposition and throw (e.g., stepping with the left foot forward as the right hand throws)
- Jumps over a 15" (38-cm) high rope
- Standing broad jump for 3'
- Copies "Simon says" postures crossing the midline
- Advanced throwing (stepping in opposition)

7 YEARS
- Crouched position on tiptoes (7.6 years)
- Arises from supine to standing position in 1–1.5 seconds
- Jumps ropes without assistance (7.6 years)
- Catches a tennis ball with one hand
- Puts coins in a box in 16 seconds
- Knows right/left concepts on self

Getting Started

Early movement experiences have a great potential to enhance a child's self-image, because the actions are so personal and because success depends so much on one's skills and abilities. For this reason, it is critical that teachers, paraprofessionals, and parents provide positive reinforcement—and lots of it—when young children attempt movement activities. Children with SI dysfunction need to move freely and with few verbal cues and environmental restrictions. Exploring movement creates an arena for children to learn new ways to move and integrate those movements into a planned motor action.

Here are some simple guidelines:

1. There is no right or wrong way for the child to respond to movement cues. Try the movement yourself before you ask the children to perform it.
2. Each movement experience is exploratory.
3. The children need to learn and move at their pace, not ours.
4. Continuity, repetition, and practice are the base for learning motor skills.
5. Music assists the child to begin and end the activity. Closure occurs with the music and helps children to develop organizational skills.
6. Administering stimulation should be done one modality at a time—aural, visual, and tactile/kinesthetic.
7. After movement experiences, ask the children to recall in words what they did with their bodies. This stimulates language and connects the motor skill with language acquisition.
8. Reverse mainstream practices have been used widely and very successfully, because mainstream children can serve as role models for children with SI dysfunction.

Making Your Classroom a Place Children Love to Be

Philosophy and Rationale

There are several reasons why large- and fine-motor activities are important in the school curriculum. From the beginning, children develop a concept of themselves by being able to move their entire bodies confidently through space.

It is vital that all children develop a strong sense of self. As they move through space, they learn what they can do with different parts of their bodies, and in this way they begin to feel their own presence and understand who they are. Body movement also lays the foundation for the development of cognitive concepts. For example, children learn what narrow and wide mean by actually moving through and touching narrow and wide spaces. For very young children, all learning begins through the body. Likewise, their self-esteem and confidence are rooted in the ability to use their bodies effectively.

Once a child gains such skills, new avenues of self-expression are open. The results can be seen in the graceful, free, and creative way more agile children use the space in a classroom. If properly designed, classroom space may, for example, set boundaries for the hyperactive child, helping him with controlled and creative activities. The classroom should also have areas both in which children can move and have quiet, personal space. Once the child begins to accept the boundaries of an area designated for large-motor play, he will gradually be able to recognize the rules and boundaries of fine-motor-task areas as well.

A Sensory-Balanced Atmosphere

Children learn as they engage in various classroom activities. Their perception of the environment is critical as they engage in cognitive and motor skills. They learn as they receive stimulus through the day and respond with the perception needed. They react to constant information received from the senses and respond as needed for an optimum result. Here are some concepts that allow a teacher to provide a sensory balanced atmosphere in the classroom. The teacher should be aware of the children as they engage in these cognitive and motor concepts:

▶ Timing—the ability to choose or the choice of the best moment to do or say something, for example, in performing music, classroom activities, or in gross motor skills

► Moving—the body's ability to coordinate body-part function as well as negotiating the body through the present environment

► Watching—being carefully observant and alert in classroom activities

► Ending—can be the final or concluding part of something; for example a book or movie, the manner in which something is ended, and/or the process of concluding a relationship with another person, especially a teacher or another child

► Connecting—to link or join two or more learning experiences, things, or people; to make a psychological or emotional association between people, things, or events; to set up a communication link between people, organizations, or places; to have a good rapport with others

► Resting—a state or period of refreshing freedom from exertion of classroom activities; the cessation of movement or action; freedom from mental or emotional anxiety; to be subject to no further discussion or attention

► Listening—to concentrate on hearing somebody or something; to pay attention to something and take it into account

► Sequencing—arranging a number of things in a particular order or connected in some way, or a number of actions or events that happen one after another; the order in which things are arranged, actions are carried out, or events happen; to arrange things or perform actions in a definite order

► Touching—to put a part of the body, especially the fingertips, in contact with something so as to feel it; to be in, or bring something into physical contact with an object; to apply the slightest pressure to something; to have an effect or influence on somebody or something; to consume something, especially food or drink, or otherwise make use of something; the sense by which the texture, shape, and other qualities are felt through contact with parts of body, especially the fingertips; the quality or combination of qualities experienced through the sensation of touch; a coming into contact with a part of the body; a light pushing or pressing stroke

► Acting—the action of carrying something out; to do something to change a situation—for example, to solve a problem or prevent one arising; to adopt a particular way of behaving; to behave in a way intended to impress other people; to serve a particular purpose or perform a particular function; to create, produce or bring about an effect or result

► Beginning—the first part or early stages of something; the point in time or space at which something starts, comes into existence, or is first encountered; the conditions in which something or somebody starts; somebody who has just started to do or learn something; to do something that was not being done before; to have as its starting point, first action, or first part, or be the starting point or first part of something; to undertake, use, or give attention to something for the first time; to start to say something, or start by saying something; to be able to succeed in accomplishing a particular task

The teacher should be aware of the environmental concepts in the classroom as they impact the children:

▶ Direction—the way in which somebody or something goes or faces
▶ Size—the amount or scope,of something, in terms of how large or small it is
▶ Proportion—the relationship between two or more parts of a whole; the correct or desirable relationship of size, quantity, or degree between two or more things or parts of something
▶ Scale—the extent or relative size of something
▶ Light—a particular kind or quality of brightness; an artificial source of illumination—for example, an electric lamp or a candle; the path that light takes; the condition of brightness created by the rays of the sun during the day; the arrival of the sun's brightness at the beginning of the day; a window or other opening in a building designed to let sunlight in; full of illumination or relatively well lighted; of a relatively pale shade; to illuminate, brighten, or shine on something; to lead or direct somebody with a source of illumination such as a flashlight; the rapid changes that occur in the eye to permit vision when moving from darkness to light
▶ Color—the property of objects that depends on the light that they reflect and is perceived as red, blue, green, or other shades; brightness and variety in the colors a room or a picture has; the property or aspect of something that involves hue, lightness, and saturation or in the space of light, hue, brightness, and saturation; the aspect of visual perception by which an observer recognizes colors; the perceived difference in a color that occur when it is surrounded by another color
▶ Texture—the feel and appearance of a surface, especially how rough or smooth it is; the structure of a substance or material such as soil or food, especially how it feels when touched or chewed; the rough quality of a surface or fabric; to give a surface a particular feel, usually one that is rough and grainy
Surface—the outermost or uppermost part of a thing, the one that is usually presented to the outside world and can be seen and touched;

a solid flat area—for example, an area on which it is suitable to work; a flat or curved continuous area definable in two dimensions Boundary—the point at which something ends or beyond which it becomes something else; the official line that divides one area from the other

► Edges—the line where two surfaces of something solid meet
► Arrangement—a group of things organized in a way that is meant to be pleasing to look at, or the arranging of such a group; the way in which something is organized; to put people or things in a position or order

As both areas are interchangeable, the child's sensory system is stimulated as follows:

► Vision—the ability to see; the whole area that can be seen by the eyes when they are kept in one direction; the creation of a clear picture of something in the mind; a clear picture of something created in the mind; the coordination of the body's visual and motor systems, such as, for example, in reaching for something being looked at; relating to or involving motor processes that are linked to vision, for example, the coordination of movement; able or intended to be seen by the eyes especially as opposed to being registered by one of the other senses; able to be perceived as a picture in the mind rather than as an abstract idea

► Touch—the sense by which the texture, shape, and other qualities of objects are felt through contact with parts of the body, especially the fingertips; the quality or combination of qualities experienced through the sensation of touch; a coming into contact with a part of the body; a light pushing or pressing stroke; to put a part of the body, especially the fingertips, in contact with something so as to feel it; to be in, or bring something into, physical contact with an object; to apply the slightest pressure to something; to consume something, especially food or drink, or otherwise make use of something; to come close to somebody or something

► Smell—to detect or recognize something by means of sensitive nerves in the nose; to use the sensitive nerves in the nose to assess something; to detect the presence or existence of something, usually something bad; the sense based on the sensitive nerves in the nose that distinguish odors; the quality of something that can be detected by sensitive nerves in the nose; an act or instance of breathing something in through the nose in order to make a judgment about it

► Auditory—relating to the sense organs, or process of hearing; the perception of sound, made possible by vibratory changes in air pressure on the eardrum; the range within which something can be heard

► Taste—the sense that perceives qualities of something such as a food by means of the sensory organs in the tongue (taste buds—a sensory receptor on the surface of the tongue that sends signals to the brain when stimulated by certain chemicals, producing the sense of taste); the sensation stimulated in the taste buds when food, drink, or other substances are in contact with them; to discern the flavor of a substance by means of the taste buds; to put a small amount of food or drink into the mouth in order to test its flavor

► Vestibular—a branch of the acoustic nerve that carries impulses from the semicircular canals and other organs to the inner ear, conveying information about posture and balance

► Body awareness—comprising of body image, body concept, and body schema. Body image refers to self-image, to how children feel about themselves. Through positive physical activities children can enhance their body image. Body concept is the knowledge of the body parts. Research shows that some children cannot identify all the body parts until the age of nine years. Body schema is the understanding of where the body parts are in relation to each other. Body schema is developed as the child engages in movement activities stimulating muscles, joints, and soft tissue.

Ordinary motor activities (walking, crawling, climbing, and swinging) coordinate vision with gross-motor tasks and responses of one or more parts of the body. The eyes gather information that is necessary in guiding the body to accomplish a job.

Fine-motor activities use delicate muscle groups, especially in the hands and fingers, to manipulate small objects. Fine-motor activities are needed for most elementary school curricula and, therefore, are the most direct avenue to success in the regular school program.

Counterpart to Fine-Motor Activity

Spatial organization (understanding different kinds of movement: walking, crawling, sliding, etc.; different positions and directions; high and low, in and out, etc; different boundaries; flat and curved, corners and edges, etc.) requires most of the same abilities as detailed tasks, such as sequencing, boundary recognition, conceptualization, and eye-hand coordination but with expanded visual, motor, and spatial involvement. Spatial organization can work either as an extender of fine-motor skills or as an introduction to them, depending on the child's needs.

Classroom environment is a critical factor in creating interactive situations in which expressive and receptive language is encouraged. Arrange the space so that eye contact and speech occur naturally and thus create many opportunities for social communication (talking).

Space for Learning

► Provide lighting that is natural or spot incandescent lamps (incandescent light is warmer and can be directed)
► Use neutral colors on work stations, such as beige or off-white; use environmental colors from objects such as leaves, bark, wood, clay, rocks, to provide good background colors for floors, walls, ceilings.
► Lighting should be adapted for the time of the year, with more light added during darker months.
► Present lessons at eye-level for child's orientation.
► Stimulation should be
   Limited: remove distractions in the classroom based on the needs of the children—how much stimulus they can or cannot tolerate. Selective: Vary the level by changing the different workstations from horizontal to vertical planes; the child learns spatially by becoming aware of himself in space in relation to his environment. As he deals with change in the environment he sees himself in that environment.
► Use materials and equipment in more than one way. Allowing the children to perform classroom activities in a variety of positions (e.g. reading at their desks, in a beanbag chair, lying on the floor) gives the children different opportunities to engage in school activities. Providing an environment in which each child can be recognized as unique creates opportunities to have their sensory needs met by positioning.
► Change the environment as frequently as possible.

Changing Space to Accommodate Learning

Factors in the Use of Space

We speak of the landscape of the classroom on purpose. Unfortunately, many classrooms are only rigid little rooms, isolated from the broad spaces of the world. The more we work with space in the classrooms, however, the more we push out the boundaries of our rooms, and the more the rooms become geography. Not isolated spaces, school classrooms can present natural spatial conditions: things near and far, high and low, horizontal and vertical. The space of classrooms is the raw material for setting up the same topographic relationships and challenges that children find in nature and in their neighborhoods.

Nonetheless, space is an elusive concept. The more complex the definition, the more infinite the idea seems to become. In the classroom, we have often limited ourselves to operational ideas of space: how space can help children learn; what role it plays in developing imagination; and what playing-field it provides for building self-image and socialization. We define space as the relationship of distance, direction, and time to the boundaries of objects, people, and places. To be successful, every child must eventually be able to recognize boundaries, to move toward and through them in useful sequence (a planned movement through the environment) and to achieve a balance between her internal and external spatial concepts. Children's sensory systems are the links between their internal and external worlds and are largely developed by their encounters with conditions external to their bodies.

Characteristics of Space in Your Classroom

Light and Color

Light is the driving force, the main energizer, of space. Space comes to life—and we come to life in space—through light. The blackouts in big cities create instant disorder and loss of function, not because humans are not used to darkness, which we need for personal renewal and catharsis, but because we can only operate outwardly when there is light. Our body systems have evolved with sunlight, a particular kind of light that provides completely for us. Artificial light is not so complete and does not give our senses all the forms of light we are set up to use. This means that, as of now, no artificial light is as good for us as sunlight.

Some forms of artificial light in widespread use are more complete (replicating natural light more closely) than others, and they are better for classroom tasks. Incandescent lighting, offset lighting, the use of filters are some examples. Whatever the artificial light source, a classroom should have as much natural light as possible. It is best for natural light to enter the room from more than one direction so that the room is not lopsided with high light intensity on one side and comparative darkness on the other. When light enters a room from two directions, it creates two spatial axes, which put the room at rest. (See illustration on page 43.) The single axis created by windows on only one wall often becomes a restless line force leading attention out of the room. Many classrooms have windows on only one side. This means that teachers must take steps to spread the light and counterbalance the power of the windows. Translucent curtains and slatted blinds can diffuse the light and direct it further into the room.

Fluorescent lighting is the least expensive and most energy-efficient form of commonly available lighting. It is difficult to convince school officials that fluorescent lighting should be used sparingly, if at all, in classroom situations. But difficult as it is, it is an issue that must be tackled.

Incandescent lighting is the only commonly available lighting that is appropriate for school spaces. It is more expensive, less energy-efficient, and requires more maintenance, but it is better quality light—not as complete as sunlight (but warmer than fluorescent), non-oscillating, quiet, and directional.

Whatever the light source, the colors of the surfaces and objects in the room will contribute strongly to the feel of the room and the conditions for seeing. When colors are bright and intense they can be draining on the eye as a steady diet. A child's eyes are constantly put to work to accommodate the movement of these colors (as the light changes throughout the day). This requires a physical change in the eye and is hard work, especially when these colors are viewed under fluorescent light. Bright colors can be used sparingly and most effectively when they appear in contrast to a neutral background.

Scale and Proportion

Light, color, and surfaces combine with the size and shape of a room to give its character or, more formally, its scale and proportion. Whether we recognize it or not, we are affected by size and balance. When we are affected positively, we will want to be in the room. When the effect is negative, we may even fear the space. If children are encouraged to describe the feel of their classroom, they often say that it does not feel right. Why?

Too many classrooms have been designed for older children and adults. In such rooms, you will notice that the windowsills, chalkboard, and coat hooks are too high and the space is not subdivided. The bottom half of the walls are painted a dark color, the furniture is too big, and the shelves are out of reach. The radiators loom large and all the lighting is on the ceiling. The room's horizon has been set high for bigger people.

Children are forced to operate in the room's "basement" when their size is not taken into the account in a room's design.

There is also the problem of an institutional look. Children feel this right away because they see a contrast to their home environment. Children note the lack of spatial variety and the hardness of the surfaces. They are used to smaller, warmer, interconnected spaces. The floor area of a classroom may be the right size to carry out a program, but the shape of the space may make the room seem unapproachable.

Traditional classrooms with 20–30 desks set up in rows can confine children's movements. Positive sensory experiences can only occur when the room arrangement is expanded to allow for movement. Desks need to be removed or set in a manner that allows free movement. Sound and temperature will affect the classroom atmosphere, as well. Children with sensory dysfunction may be challenged simply by the negative stimuli they receive every day. Setting up the classroom in a nontraditional arrangement is high priority for alert teachers.

Global Movement Experience

Global movement, which involves moving the whole body at the same time, can enhance every child's school performance. These movements assist children to succeed in school because of the following benefits.

▶ Improve physical coordination.

▶ Develop body awareness, comprising of body image, body concept, and body schema. Body image refers to self-image. Body image refers to how children feel about themselves. Through positive physical activities children can enhance their body images. Body concept is the knowledge of the body parts.

▶ Develop body schema, the understanding of where the body parts are in relation to each other. Body schema is developed as the child engages in movement activities stimulating muscles, joints, and soft tissue.

▶ Improve children's attention spans by engaging in movements that strengthen aural comprehension and visual perception skills.

▶ Develop realistic self-esteem.

What to Do

A. **Give Simple Movement Directions:** Young children may find it difficult to follow movements that combine spoken, visual, and hands-on directions. Therefore, as you introduce activities, simplify your presentations by using only one of these methods at a time. To discover if the children understand what you are trying to convey, ask them questions about it after you have finished describing, demonstrating, or guiding.

B. **Have the Children Describe the Completed Movements:** Teachers may pose problems and then ask questions to help the children become even more aware of their physical movements and their developing body coordination. You can help your students become aware of the parts of their bodies, the movements those parts of the body can perform, and what their bodies can do in space. This is called kinesthetic awareness.

Teachers can
(1) talk about a movement while doing it,
(2) plan and then execute a movement,
(3) recall a completed movement, and
(4) link a single movement to a single word.

C. **Have the Children Move in Stationary Positions:** Children can perform these activities in one place without moving around; i.e., do the movement in a personal space or self-space. These involve movements of the upper and lower body in any non-weight-bearing position, or movements of the body while standing without transferring weight from one foot to the other. Children become aware of how their bodies can move without traveling through space.

D. **Have the Children Move in Different Ways Throughout the Classroom:** Locomotor movements require one to travel through space, either horizontally or vertically. Variations are virtually the same as those for nonlocomotor movements. When engaged in locomotor movement, children learn to use their bodies in many different ways. The goals are to help them
(1) develop an awareness of how their bodies move about;
(2) understand the language used to describe locomotor movement;
(3) develop improved balance, so that they can start and stop adequately;
(4) develop improved coordination, so movements can be sequenced;
(5) feel comfortable about moving.

E. **Have the Children Move with Objects:** Young children need opportunities to move with objects (balls, balloons, beanbags, and so forth). These provide opportunities for them to use motor coordination in new ways and to develop comfort with objects. They need chances to manipulate objects on their own rather than working with partners or in small groups.

F. **Have the Children Move in Creative Ways:** Express creativity in movement by taking any nonlocomotor or locomotor movement, with or without objects, and change that movement in some way. This is often is very threatening to children. Until they are comfortable with movement and know what their bodies can do, they cannot express creativity in movement. Use these three modes to assist the children to be creative: simple problem solving, guided exploration, and imagery.

Intervention Strategies for SI Dysfunction

Getting It Together

When sensory issues begin to hinder and affect the child's education, classroom teachers can select appropriate strategies. Sensory-motor activities should be carefully planned with the consultation of the occupational therapist, physical therapist, and adapted PE specialist, who work closely with the child. It is important to select an activity that the child can engage in easily for her developmental stage. Sensory integration and recreation activities will help the child with SI dysfunction.

When working with a child with a suspected integration problem, the teacher should have a copy of the Pre-referral Motor Screening Checklist (see pages 48-52) to keep a record of the characteristics observed in the classroom. As this checklist is completed (it can be done over a period of days or weeks) the teacher can share this information with the I.E.P. (Individual Education Plan) team members (special education teacher, occupational therapist, physical therapist, speech/language pathologists, etc.) for further observations and determination of sensory problems. This process of assessment allows teachers to understand the nature and scope of the sensory problems and, more importantly, provides current information to help select the proper strategies for intervention.

The Intervention Strategies pages should be reproduced so that the classroom teacher can have easy access to the activities. It is highly suggested that only a few strategies be selected when beginning an intervention program. Each activity should be provided to the child for exposure and experience. The teacher needs to be aware of the present level of functioning of the child and in turn then monitor the progress of the child engaging in the selected strategy (this process can and should take weeks). If no progress can be observed, the teacher and I.E.P. team members should reconvene, discuss, and select different strategies based on the information they have collected. This process should continue as long as progress can be determined. However, if the appropriate strategies have been selected and appropriate time was given for the child to interact with the strategies and no progress can be noted, the I.E.P. team should meet and discuss potential evaluations and strategies.

Child's Name:_____

Room: _____   School:

Pre-Referral Motor Screening Checklist
The child with SI dysfunction will show some or all of these symptoms:

Excessively Distracted by Tactile Stimulation
- ❏ Dislikes light touch or being touched at all
- ❏ Overreacts to unexpected touch or sound
- ❏ Unable to calm down after motor activity
- ❏ Avoids "getting messy" in glue, sand, finger paint, tape
- ❏ Displays unusual need for touching certain toys, surfaces, or textures
- ❏ Has decreased awareness of pain or temperature
- ❏ Other:_____

Sensory Functioning/Movement
- ❏ Pushes, shoves, kicks as a way of touching others
- ❏ Prefers touching rather then being touched
- ❏ Cannot find body parts with eyes closed
- ❏ Fearful of movement (e.g., going up and down stairs)
- ❏ Never gets dizzy (craves spinning and rolling)
- ❏ Gets dizzy easily (avoids spinning and rolling)
- ❏ Becomes anxious or distressed when feet leave the ground
- ❏ Fears falling
- ❏ Dislikes head being upside down
- ❏ Avoids climbing and jumping
- ❏ Takes excessive risks while playing, has no safety awareness
- ❏ Seeks all kinds of movement which interferes with daily life
- ❏ Avoids playground equipment or moving toys
- ❏ Rocks body without realizing it
- ❏ Twirls or spins self frequently during the day
- ❏ Other:_____

Auditory Sensations
- ❏ Overly sensitive to noise
- ❏ Misses sounds
- ❏ Likes to make loud sounds
- ❏ Has hearing loss
- ❏ Holds hands over ears
- ❏ Cannot work with background noise
- ❏ Seems oblivious within an active environment
- ❏ Other:_____

Unusual Taste And Smell Patterns
❑ Routinely smells non-food objects
❑ Seeks out certain tastes or smells
❑ Has difficulty identifying objects by touch alone
❑ Mouths objects excessively
❑ Other:_____

Poor Posture
❑ Holds head to one side
❑ Shoulder—one higher than other
❑ Hip—one higher than other
❑ Bowlegged
❑ Knock-kneed
❑ Slouches
❑ Other:_____

Weakness or Floppiness of Arms or Legs
❑ Cannot easily get up from the floor or a chair
❑ Has trouble going up or down stairs
❑ Has weaker or stronger than normal grasp
❑ Tires easily, has poor endurance
❑ Cannot lift heavy objects
❑ Other:_____

Unusual Walking Pattern
❑ Limps
❑ Feet turn in or out excessively
❑ Walks on toes
❑ Walks on heels
❑ Drags one leg
❑ Moves stiffly
❑ Other:_____

Clumsiness, Poor Coordination
❑ Poor awareness of space
❑ Poor balance
❑ Falls easily
❑ Runs into chairs, desks
❑ Has trouble catching, kicking, or throwing a ball
❑ Cannot learn new motor activities or games
❑ Behind others in motor skill development
❑ Poor use of one side of the body
❑ Makes facial grimaces or uncontrolled movements when working
❑ Other:_____

Trouble with Attention/Excessive Restlessness
❑ Cannot sit still
❑ Lethargic at times
❑ Stares blankly on occasion
❑ Frequently misses directions
❑ Has wandering eyes; cannot focus
❑ Avoids eye contact
❑ Does not notice when people come into the room
❑ Jumps from one activity to another frequently
❑ Other:_____

Fine-Motor Problems
❑ Difficulty manipulating small objects (pegs, beads, coins)
❑ Difficulty using scissors, coloring, writing, etc.
❑ Abnormal pencil grip (holds tightly or weakly, immature grasp)
❑ Jerky or tremor-like motions in hands when drawing
❑ Difficulty staying on lines when tracing
❑ Eyes do not follow hands or seem to wander
❑ Difficulty using isolated finger movements (uses arm and hand as one unit)
❑ Other:_____

Visual-Perceptual Problems
❑ Has a diagnosed visual defect
❑ Poor understanding of spatial concepts (large, small, and numerical)
❑ Poor directional concepts (up, down, right, left, in, out)
❑ Has difficulty putting puzzles together
❑ Has difficulty recognizing shapes and colors
❑ Has difficulty identifying object from the background
❑ Shows poor spacing on work papers
❑ Reverses letters, numbers, words, or phrases
❑ Shows difficulty with eye tracking
❑ Is bothered by bright lights
❑ Other:_____

Bilateral Integration Problems
❑ Avoids or has difficulty performing tasks which require eyes or extremities to cross the midline of the body
❑ Neglects or seems unaware of one side of her/his body
❑ Does not stabilize paper while writing
❑ Seems to ignore one-half of page
❑ Has an inconsistent hand dominance
❑ Regularly uses both hands together
❑ Other:_____

Learning Behaviors

❑ Short attention span
❑ Difficulty with a change in routine
❑ Difficulty recognizing own errors
❑ Difficulty working independently
❑ Slow worker
❑ Easily distracted
❑ Perseveres far too long
❑ Disorganized, messy
❑ Talks aloud, hums, sings
❑ Rushes through work
❑ Other:_____

Social/Emotional Problems

❑ Verbally aggressive
❑ Behavior bothers others
❑ Happiest playing alone; isolates self from others
❑ Physically aggressive
❑ Attention-seeking
❑ Impulsive
❑ Lacks confidence
❑ Cries easily
❑ Fearful of new situations
❑ Easily frustrated
❑ Falls asleep in class
❑ Cannot calm down
❑ Has difficulty making friends
❑ Is overly serious
❑ Does not express emotions
❑ Other:_____

Activities of Daily Living

❑ Has trouble dressing/undressing (or fastening, buttoning, zipping, tying shoes)
❑ Needs assistance when toileting
❑ Has trouble grooming (brushing teeth, washing face, etc.)
❑ Has trouble eating (e.g., bringing food to the mouth, chewing and swallowing, sucking with a straw, drinking from a cup)
❑ Drools:
  ❑ Always   ❑ Under stress   ❑ Only when eating
❑ Avoids certain textures of foods
❑ Other:_____

Pain or Discomfort
❑ Unusual or chronic complaints
❑ Other:_____

Breathing Problems
❑ Difficulty breathing even at rest
❑ Becomes short of breath after slight exercise
❑ Chronic congestion
❑ Other:_____

Orthopedic Equipment
❑ Needs braces, wheelchair, crutches, or other appliances
❑ Or, you feel student may benefit from some of these appliances
Specify: _____

_____

_____

Other Problems That Affect Learning:

_____

_____

_____

Comments or Additional Observations:

_____

_____

_____

Any Known Medications:

_____

Child's Physician: _____
Phone: _____

Any Known Surgeries: _____

_____

_____

Child's Physician: _____
Phone: _____

Any Known Seizures: _____If Yes, Type: _____
Frequency: _____
Child's Physician: _____
Phone: _____

Preparation for Handling the Special Needs Child

The classroom teacher has a phenomenal challenge to meet the needs of all the students in the classroom. The child with sensory dysfunction presents a distinct challenge. Knowledge of the characteristics and understanding the learning styles of the child is critical. Time and energy must be spent to become familiar with the child's strengths and weaknesses. Providing curriculum at the pace of the average student in the classroom may still pose a problem for the child with sensory problems.

The following suggestions provide the classroom teacher with tools to become more knowledgeable and better prepared to educate the child with sensory problems in the inclusive classroom.

1. Become familiar with all the child's records.

2. At the beginning of the school year, meet with the parents formally to discuss short-term goals and objectives for their child.

3. Seek medical records. Many times these records provide different types of information than school records.

4. Inquire about specialists (occupational therapist, physical therapist) with whom parents are in contact who may have information to assist you. You will need to obtain parent permission for the release of such information.

5. Contact therapists and/or the speech and language pathologists to receive information that will assist you in your preparation of activities, strategies, and techniques that you will use with your new student.

6. Include your paraprofessional in all meetings with and without parents. Due to the number of students in your class, your paraprofessional often becomes the child's "shadow" or will have worked closely with the child on various tasks. Therefore, the paraprofessional should have equal access to all information regarding the child's educational needs.

7. Plan to meet biweekly or as needed with all the school personnel who will be working with your student. Include and share all strategies and techniques that were successful or unsuccessful. Children need a tremendous amount of consistency in their day.

8. Ask your administrator for professional days to attend conferences, to observe other similar programs, and to meet with outside consultants who may have expertise in the education of children with sensory dysfunction within school systems. Once again you will need to inservice your paraprofessional on this material and information you receive in order to maintain consistency in the child's program.

9. Due to the difficulties with processing sensory input, the child can have a difficult time learning in a classroom with a high presentation of stimuli. Therefore, it is highly recommended to prepare your classroom by reducing sources of possible stimuli around the room, on the walls, lights, colors, etc. (See page 19.)

10. Begin to plan how you can use classmates to serve as role models, displaying normal behaviors for the child. Think of ways these students can provide "normal" language, motor, and/or social emotional modeling of behavior.

11. Plan each day's events carefully to provide calm transition times for the child. Be sure to communicate when a transition time will take place to prepare the child for the change in routine. Keep in mind not to be too rigid when your student has a high level of energy during certain periods of the day. At that time you need to "run with the child" and get back to your schedule later.

12. Encourage parents to assist their child by creating a room or an area in their home in which it will be a stimuli-reduced area. This area can be used for the child to regroup and/or a place for learning new things or practicing specific skills.

13. Give special attention to seating arrangements in the classroom. Have the student sit close and in direct eye contact with the teacher. More importantly, be aware of the figure-ground stimuli that affect the student. Background stimuli on the front wall and nearby walls can be distracting. The student may be drawn to visual stimulus instead of focusing on auditory stimulus, such as when you give directions for an activity. Similarly, when children with special needs begin to look at picture books, they tend to pick out one small piece of the whole, probably because they cannot take in the meaning of the whole scene.

Implementing a Strategy

When analyzing the child's special needs, consider the following suggestions as you select intervention strategies and plan worthwhile learning experiences:

- Provide ample time for the child to experience the activity (allow for repetition) and give the child time to build upon this task (continuity).

- Allow the child to practice the skills of the activity along with another activity that demands the same skills.

- Use various media and senses. Add or subtract sensory information. Questions to consider:

   Is there too much auditory or visual stimulation as the child engages in the activity?
   Is the activity tactually distracting?

- Follow developmental progressions and adjust the level of the skill accordingly.

- Break the task down into parts. Do one part at a time. Allow the child to complete the parts in short periods.

- Modify the task so that the child is able to finish it and get a sense of accomplishment and confidence in completing a task.

Suggested Equipment and Supplies

As the teacher becomes familiar with the numerous intervention activities listed on the following pages, many common classroom supplies (e.g. scissors, staples, etc.) may need to be located. Consult your P.E. teacher, physical therapist, and occupational therapist when selecting these items. The various pieces of equipment can be found in catalogs and local stores. Included in this list are some supplies that may not be commonly found in the classroom but are important instructional tools for engaging children in these interventions:

- T-stool

- Therapy ball (16–24 inch or 40–61 cm size)

- Beanbag chairs (different sizes)
- Therapy bands (different strengths)
- Bungee cords

- Sandpaper (different grits)
- Weighted vest

- Bolsters (different sizes)

- Sandbags (different weights)
- Wall mirror

- Board games
- Tape recorder
- Chewy candy
- Chewing gum
- Rubber tubing
- Latex gloves
- Vibrating pens
- Pencil grips
- Carpet samples
- Chopsticks
- Chenille stems
- Modeling clay and play clay
- Drinking straws
- Felt
- Reclining lawn chairs
- Clothespins
- Medicine droppers
- Incandescent lamps
- Slant board
- Mats (personal size)
- Spring-loaded paper clips
- Weighted mitts
- Spongy balls
- Bubble wrap

- Marbles
- Playing cards
- Nuts and bolts (various sizes)
- Crazy foam
- Shaving cream
- Whipping cream
- Pudding
- Hand cream
- Earplugs
- Headphones
- Office chair
- Scooter board
- Rice, cornmeal
- Tactile bin
- Graph paper
  (for spatial orientation)
- Magnet clips
- Jacks
- Bubble solution
- Color-coding paper
- Flashlights
- Super-bounce balls
- Lacing cards with strings
- Beanbags

General Considerations That Apply for All Types of SI Dysfunction

When planning activities and specific strategies for the child with special needs, incorporate or consider some of the following general suggestions.

_____ Consider mental age, environmental background, and previous activity experiences when selecting activities.

_____ Be aware of the language understanding level of the child when giving verbal instructions.

_____ Correlate physical education activities with classroom activities to provide reinforcement of academic concepts.

_____ Keep the environment simple and free from outside noises and distractions.

_____ Emphasize vocal and motor "output modalities" that are generated during activities. For example, have the child describe what he is doing as he is encouraged to move through the environment.

_____ Use class games to practice body-part identification, laterality, directionality, listening skills, and midline crossing activities.

_____ Read stories aloud and ask children to describe and act out what a certain person in the story did. Ask them to finish a story for you through actions and words.

_____ Use a kinesthetic approach along with clear, concise descriptions when introducing new skills.

_____ Offer as many socially appropriate ways of making physical contact during the day as possible (e.g., shaking hands, "high five," pat on the back).

_____ Do not cover too much in one session.

_____ Use story plays (excellent means for a child to practice listening skills).

_____ Read poetry aloud to children, stopping frequently to allow them to finish the phrases with rhyming words.

_____ Allow the child to practice and repeat skills for the pleasure of doing something successfully.

Poor Posture

If One or More of These Characteristics Are Exhibited . . .

- ❏ Head held to one side
- ❏ Shoulder: one higher than other
- ❏ Hip: one higher than other
- ❏ Bowlegged
- ❏ Knock-kneed
- ❏ Slouches

Try These Activities

(Some activities incorporate more than one sensory skill and are listed under the categories that apply.)

Vestibular

____ With hands and knees on the floor, have the child balance on two legs and one arm, two arms and one leg, and then on just one leg and one arm.

____ Hang a rope swing outdoors, using an old tire or a disk. Have the child swing and spin around while exploring a variety of positions, such as sitting, leaning, and arching backwards.

Motor Planning

____ Have the child lie on her back and put her hands in her pockets. Encourage her to wiggle through a hoop as if she were a caterpillar by using trunk movements, not arms or hands. Then have the child lie on her stomach and do the same. (Also Proprioceptive)

Bilateral Motor Coordination

____ Allow the child to erase chalk- or whiteboard.

____ Have the child swing, lift, and rotate his arms and legs.

____ Practice the knee walk on a carpet-sample pathway. Have the child grasp ankles behind back as she walks on her knees.

Proprioceptive/Kinesthetic

_____ Have the child lie on his back and curl into the tuck position, holding this position for 30 seconds. Then have the child lie on his stomach and come up into the airplane position, with head, arms, and legs lifted up off the floor; hold this for 30 seconds.

_____ Wall push-ups—the child does these with head facing the wall; the goal is to touch the nose to the wall.

_____ Practice crab-walk relays.

_____ Have the child lie on her stomach over a large ball and then put her hands on the floor in front of it. Encourage the child to walk hands forward as far as possible, keeping the body stiff.

Equilibrium

_____ Allow the child to stand while working at desk.

_____ Walk while balancing a book on the head.

_____ Walk on toes forward and backward, carrying a heavy object.

_____ Arrange several inner tubes in a straight line. Have the child walk with one foot on an inner tube and the other off the tube.

General Suggestions

_____ Have the child maintain a hands-and-knees position on the floor while you gently try to push him over to one side or the other. Push to the left and right while encouraging the child not to let you knock him down.

Clumsiness, Poor Coordination

If One or More of These Characteristics Are Exhibited . . .

- ❏ Poor awareness of space
- ❏ Poor balance
- ❏ Falls easily
- ❏ Runs into chairs and desks
- ❏ Has trouble catching, kicking, or throwing a ball
- ❏ Cannot learn new motor activities or games
- ❏ Behind others in motor skills
- ❏ Poor use of one side of the body
- ❏ Makes facial grimaces or uncontrolled movements when working

Try These Activities

(Some activities incorporate more than one sensory/motor skill and are listed under the categories that apply.)

Vestibular

_____ Have the child move through classroom in novel ways, e.g., walking backwards/sideways, hopping, crawling.

_____ Have the child sit on T-stool or therapy ball.

_____ Encourage the child to move in different directions and in various ways to develop dynamic and static balance.

Tactile

_____ Encourage the child to crawl, scoot, roll, or "commando/army crawl" on different types of surfaces.

_____ Have the child roll like a log on carpet mats, foam mats, and other textures to supply the desired touch/pressure input.

_____ Roll a large ball over the child while she lies in prone or supine position.

_____ Have the child squeeze/pinch clay prior to a writing activity.

_____ Have the child wear a heavy backpack.

_____ Provide kinesthetic cues that may range from a signal, such as a tap on the shoulder, to leading the children actually through the movement.

_____ Spread a large blanket on the floor. Have the child lie on it and then roll like a log to wrap the blanket around his body.

Motor Planning

_____ Give the child a desk at both the front and back of the room so she can move between class activities.

_____ Have the child move through the classroom in novel ways; e.g., walking backwards/sideways, hopping, crawling.

_____ Allow children enough room to have some freedom of movement but make the area confining enough to maintain order and interest.

_____ Encourage children to work and move in space to be aware of their relationship to others and their environment.

_____ Provide the child with rich experiences in manipulating his environment.

_____ Secure child's pencil box with interlocking plastic strips to the desk to decrease accidental dropping.

_____ Emphasize vocal and motor "output modalities" that are generated during activities. For example, have the child describe what she is doing, as she is encouraged to move through the environment.

_____ Use class games to practice body-part identification, laterality, directionality, listening skills, and midline crossing activities. (Also Bilateral Motor Coordination)

_____ Read stories aloud and ask children to describe and act out what a certain person in the story did. Ask them to finish a story for you through actions and words.

_____ Have children move their heads, shoulders, arms, hands, or trunks while sitting or lying.

_____ Encourage the children to bend, stretch, twist, turn, and shake as many body parts of their bodies as possible while standing, sitting, or lying on a mat.

_____ Walk while bending one part of the body; repeat in various ways.

Bilateral Motor Coordination

_____ Have the child squeeze/pinch clay prior to a writing activity.

_____ Have the child cut materials such as clay, straws, sandpaper, oak tag, and felt. (Also Tactile)

_____ Have the child use a stapler or hole puncher on sheets of paper. (Also Tactile)

_____ Practice the knee walk on a carpet-sample pathway. Have the child grasp her ankles behind back as she walks on her knees.

_____ Have the child do modified push-ups and chin-ups.

_____ Encourage the child to roll a large ball using even thrusts.

_____ Practice the wheelbarrow walk by walking on hands while the feet are held off the floor by a partner.

_____ Allow the child to choose alternate positions for working; e.g., on stomach on floor, curled up in corner, etc.

_____ Have the child push a beanbag along a path while crawling or moving body with the commando/army crawl.

Proprioceptive/Kinesthetic

_____ Have the child assist with moving classroom furniture. Try smaller items first and progress to larger and heavier ones as the child seems able.

_____ Have the child sit in a chair backwards so that the legs straddle the seat and the chest is against the back of the chair.

_____ Allow the child to choose alternate positions for working; e.g., on stomach on floor, curled up in corner, etc.

_____ Have the child sit upright in chair while keeping feet flat on floor.

_____ Use resistive activities; e.g., pull back on the person's arm as she tries to bring it forward.

_____ Provide proprioceptive activities (i.e. pushing, pulling, and squeezing) prior to fine motor activities.

_____ Have the child squeeze/pinch clay prior to a writing activity.

_____ Wrap a bungee cord/therapy band around front two legs of a chair and have the child use his legs to stretch out the cord or band.

_____ Incorporate deep-pressure exercises into daily routine:
- ► shifting weight from side to side when sitting
- ► pressing hands together
- ► putting hands on top of head and pressing down
- ► crossing arms and press on shoulders with opposite hand
- ► putting hands on knees and pressing down
- ► putting hands under opposite elbows and press up
- ► rotating shoulders and then upper trunk side to side
- ► tilting head rhythmically side to side
- ► brushing hands down arms firmly

_____ Weigh down school supplies such as pencil boxes, notebooks, etc., with washers or plaster of Paris.

_____ Suggest that the child wear tight-fitting clothing such as tights, spandex, suspenders or a weighted vest. (Also Tactile)

_____ Have the child wear a heavy backpack.

_____ Have the child sit on hands.

_____ Provide deep pressure touch to hyperactive/distractible child periodically throughout the day.

_____ Place sandbags, beanbags, or bolsters on child's lap when appropriate, if needed.

_____ Use maximum stimuli such as the following in teaching new skills.

► Kinesthetic stimuli: guide the child's body parts through desired movement for a physical sense of the pattern.

► Tactile stimuli: use touch to relate more effectively to the child which part of the body is to be used; also, the child may learn more about the equipment and environment by touch.

► Visual stimuli: use visual aids such as slides, diagrams, demonstrations, pictures, films, and mirrors; be aware that mirrors may confuse right and left concepts.

Verbal stimuli: give oral instructions as the child performs.

_____ Let students put their hands on your shoulders or hips or be led physically so they receive the kinesthetic feeling of the following concepts:

► Time—show fast, slow, or uneven time by running or walking with the students.

► Space—lead the student around so she understands distances and the area of the classroom.

► Size—physically show the students how to be tall, short, or wide, and relate this to their environment.

_____ Provide kinesthetic cues, which may range from a signal, such as a tap on the shoulder, to actually leading the children through the movement.

_____ Using a strong rope, children play "tug of war," trying to pull the other team across a line.

_____ Have students push and pull using elbows, arms, hands, and trunk while lying, sitting, or standing.

_____ Have children bend, stretch, twist, turn, and shake as many body parts of the body as possible while standing, sitting, or lying.

Equilibrium

_____ Have the child sit in a chair backwards so that the legs straddle the seat and the chest is against the back of the chair. (Also Proprioceptive/Kinesthetic)

_____ Have the child sit upright in a chair while still having feet flat on floor. (Also Proprioceptive/Kinesthetic)

_____ Invite the child to sit on T-stool or therapy ball.

_____ Encourage the children to move in different directions and in various ways to develop dynamic and static balance.

_____ Provide opportunities for the child to walk on stilts and bounce on a pogostick.

_____ Have the child play hopscotch.

Case Study

Tommy's first-grade teacher had been concerned earlier in the year about his ability to move in the classroom, at recess, and throughout the building. She often talked with the P.E. teacher concerning Tommy's gross motor skills. He exhibits poor balance, always falling; he has trouble catching, kicking, and playing simple movement games with his friends. His self-esteem appears to be in jeopardy. He appears to be a bright young boy with learning potential; however, these characteristics displayed throughout the school day have impeded his opportunities to learn. After further discussion with the P.E. teacher and others (art and music teachers), the Pre-Referral Motor Screening Checklist was filled out. The adapted physical education (A.P.E.) specialist began observing Tommy in P.E. classes and at recess. Each observation concluded that Tommy indeed was behind in his gross motor skill development. Further observations indicated that Tommy might also have low muscle tone (hypotonia). The A.P.E. Specialist wants the physical therapist to observe Tommy so has recommended a Child Study to discuss Tommy's program in depth.

At the Child Study, his teacher, P.E. teacher, school psychologist, A.P.E. specialist, physical therapist, and principal attended. Information was provided in writing from Tommy's art and music teachers describing his progress and movements in their classes. After collecting information from the Child Study, it was agreed that Tommy may have a delay in his gross motor skills that was impacting his education. Therefore, the Child Study Team recommended an I.E.P. (Individualized Education Program) meeting with his parents to discuss possible evaluations. At that meeting, it was recommended that the physical therapist evaluate Tommy's muscle tone and gross motor abilities.

As this evaluation was being conducted, the following general suggestions and activities were given to the teacher as intervention strategies:

1) Correlate physical education activities with classroom activities to provide reinforcement of academic concepts, such as "Alphabet Relay." This simple relay game incorporates gross motor development skills (locomotor skills) and academic concepts. The children can be divided into four to five groups sitting on the floor in a line on one side of the classroom, gym, or playing area. On the opposite side of the area are piles of laminated alphabet letters placed in front of each line. On command, the first child of each line performs a locomotor skill (hops) to the pile of mixed-up letters, finds the "A," and returns performing the same locomotor skill. The second child continues and finds the "B." The process continues until the first group completes the task of stacking the alphabet. Throughout the game, the teacher can change the locomotor skill on command. Being a part of small groups, Tommy and other children will receive the benefits from physical activity as well as academic stimulation.

2) Have Tommy assist in moving heavy objects, furniture, etc. throughout the day. He can carry books back to the library and/or perform other physically related tasks in the classroom.

3) To stimulate equilibrium reactions, have Tommy sit on a T-stool periodically throughout the day. Appropriate times may be when the children are listening to the teacher read a story, when a visitor comes to speak to the class, and/or watching a movie or demonstration.

4) Encourage Tommy to work and move in his personal space and in turn to be aware of the space others occupy by assisting him in developing a workstation.

5) Use kinesthetic stimulation when necessary to "guide" Tommy's body parts through a new learning experience. For example, when Tommy plays at recess with his friends, often he will not be able to catch a ball thrown to him. To provide kinesthetic stimulation, the teacher can stand behind Tommy and hold his wrists/hands, helping him to bring the hands together to catch when the ball is thrown.) Repeating this stimulation can begin to assist Tommy in understanding his body parts, "muscle memory," eye-hand coordination, and visual tracking. All of these skills are needed to engage in simple play activities. They are useful to transfer to the academic setting.

The physical therapist completed the evaluation and the I.E.P. team reconvened. The outcome indicated that Tommy certainly does have low muscle tone, which in turn has caused many of the gross motor development delays. It was recommended by the physical therapist to incorporate the following:

1) Keep the environment simple and allow freedom of movement by providing greater space in the classroom.

2) Encourage Tommy and others to move from one place to another by using locomotor skills rather than just walking.

3) Provide low-level games that require Tommy to be in anti-gravity positions and weight-bearing positions (bear walk, bunny hop, crawling, etc.).

4) Provide proprioceptive activities prior to fine motor activities (i.e., pushing, pulling, squeezing).

5) Use classroom games to practice body-part identification, laterality, directionality, listening skills, and midline crossing activities. These activities and skills will enhance Tommy's body awareness and in turn his self-image.

6) Attend another section of physical education during the week with another first grade class. He can bring a "friend" from his class to attend with him.

7) Encourage the family to participate in a home program that encourages physical activity each day (e.g., family walk around the neighborhood, taking Tommy to a playground, bike riding, swimming, etc.)

The I.E.P. meeting concluded and the recommendations were accepted and followed. Tommy has shown progress in his gross motor development. Activities are constantly provided for him and his classmates that require physical components to be developed. Most importantly, Tommy's self-esteem has improved.

Excessive Restlessness

If One or More of These Characteristics Are Exhibited . . .

❏ Cannot sit still but needs to move
❏ Fidgets excessively while sitting
❏ Other: _____

Try These Activities
(Some activities incorporate more than one sensory-motor skill and are listed under the categories that apply.)

Vestibular

_____ Have the child move through classroom in novel ways; e.g., walking backwards/sideways, hopping, and crawling.
_____ Have children move in different directions and in various ways to develop dynamic and static balance.
_____ Have the child sit on T-stool or therapy ball.

Tactile

_____ Provide a tactile bin in the classroom for "down time."
_____ Trace sandpaper letters with an index finger. (Also Motor Planning)
_____ Trace letter shapes on carpet samples with index finger. (Also Motor Planning)
_____ Squeeze a small balloon filled with flour.
_____ Have the child draw letters in sand, finger paint, pudding, or shaving cream.
_____ Form letters with chenille stems or clay.
_____ Provide proprioceptive activities (pushing, pulling, and squeezing) prior to fine motor activities.
_____ Allow the child to rub his hand or arm with a cloth towel.
_____ Provide kinesthetic cues, which may range from a signal such as a tap on the shoulder to leading the child actually through the movement.
_____ Draw shapes on a carpet sample. Have the child erase the marks using her hands, forearms, or bare feet.
_____ Have the child erase/wash chalkboards.
_____ Have the child squeeze/pinch clay prior to writing activity.
_____ Have the child chew chewy candy, gum, rubber tubing, etc.

Motor Planning

_____ Encourage the child to move like different animals; e.g., crab, bear, ostrich, frog, inchworm.

_____ Draw letters in flattened clay with a pencil or chopstick.

_____ Have the children do "mystery writing" at chalkboard with their eyes closed. Guide their hands to write letters or words and then have them guess what they wrote.

_____ Encourage the children to bend, stretch, twist, turn, and shake as many parts of their bodies as possible while standing, sitting, or lying.

_____ Have the child form letters with chenille stems or clay.

_____ Give the child a desk at both front and back of the room so she can move between class activities.

_____ Have the child move through classroom in novel ways; e.g., walking backwards/sideways, hopping, and crawling.

_____ Have children move their heads, shoulders, arms, hands, or trunks while sitting or lying.

_____ Teach students how to relax using yoga techniques.

_____ Allow children enough room to have some freedom of movement but make the area confining enough to maintain order and interest in the activity.

_____ Provide ample opportunities for children to express themselves in creative drama and to demonstrate their perception of the environment around them.

Bilateral Motor Coordination

_____ Pull masking tape off wall.

_____ Erase or wash chalkboards.

_____ Cut materials such as clay, straws, sandpaper, oak tag, and felt.

_____ Use a stapler or hole puncher on sheets of scrap paper. (Tactile)

_____ Secure papers together using spring-loaded paper clips. (Tactile)

_____ Squeeze/pinch clay prior to writing activity.

_____ Wear weighted mitts intermittently during writing (under supervision from therapist).

Proprioceptive/Kinesthetic

_____ Provide deep-pressure touch periodically throughout the day to a hyperactive/distractible child.

_____ Have the child sit in chair backwards so that the legs straddle the seat and the chest is against the back of the chair.

_____ Allow the child to choose alternate positions for working; e.g., on stomach on floor, curled up in corner, etc. (Also Tactile)

_____ Encourage the child to play catch at a close range with a partner, tossing a medicine ball or beanbag back and forth.

_____ Place a weighted backpack on the child's back and then pretend to "hike" to a designated area.

_____ Give the child a small rubber ball or sponge to squeeze.

_____ Teach students how to relax using yoga techniques.

_____ Have the child assist with moving classroom furniture. Try smaller items first and progress to larger and heavier ones as the child is able.

_____ Have students push and pull using elbows, arms, hands, and trunks while lying, sitting, or standing.

_____ Have the child squeeze/pinch clay prior to writing activity.

_____ Wrap bungee cord/theraband around front two legs of chair so that child can push against it with her legs.

_____ Have the child wear weighted mitts intermittently during writing (under supervision from therapist).

_____ Suggest that child wear tight-fitting clothing, e.g., tights, spandex, suspenders, or a weighted vest. (Also Tactile)

_____ Have the child wear heavy backpack.

_____ Have the child sit on hands.

_____ Have the child push palms together.

_____ Have the child use a vibrating pen for "fun writing experience."

_____ Encourage the child to deliver books to the library.

_____ Place sandbags, bean bags, or bolsters on child's lap when appropriate.

_____ Incorporate deep pressure exercises into daily routine:
- ► shifting weight in sitting from side to side
- ► pressing hands together
- ► putting hands on top of head and pressing down
- ► crossing arms and press on shoulders with opposite hands
- ► putting hands on knees and pressing down
- ► putting hands under opposite elbows and press up
- ► rotating shoulders and then upper trunk side to side
- ► tilting head rhythmically side to side
- ► brushing hands down arms firmly

_____ Have the child chew chewy candy, gum, rubber tubing, etc.

_____ Use maximum stimuli such as the following in teaching new skills:
- ► Kinesthetic stimuli: guiding of body parts through desired movement for a physical sense or feeling of the pattern
- ► Tactile stimuli: use touch to relate more effectively to the child which part of the body is to be used; also, the child may learn more about equipment and environment by touch

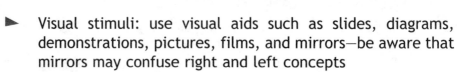

> ▶ Visual stimuli: use visual aids such as slides, diagrams, demonstrations, pictures, films, and mirrors—be aware that mirrors may confuse right and left concepts
> ▶ Verbal stimuli: give oral instructions as the child performs

_____ Let students put their hands on your shoulders or hips or be led physically so they receive the kinesthetic feeling of the following concepts:

> ▶ Time—show fast, slow, or uneven time by running or walking with the students.
> ▶ Space—lead the students around so they understand distances and the area of the classroom.
> ▶ Size—physically show the students how to be tall, short, or wide, and relate this to their environment.

Equilibrium

_____ Have the child sit in chair backwards so that the legs straddle the seat and the chest is against the back of the chair.

_____ Have children move in different directions and in various ways to develop dynamic and static balance.

_____ Allow the child to stand while working on tasks.

_____ Pretending that a wide line on the floor is a balance beam, the child walks forward heel to toe, forward on heels, backward toe to heel, sideways with a crossover step, or tiptoes forward.

_____ Encourage child to sit upright in chair and keep feet flat on floor.

General Suggestions

_____ Give short and simple instructions.

_____ If discipline is a problem, perhaps the activity is too difficult to understand, requires too much skill, has too many rules, or has too many verbal instructions.

_____ Do not frustrate the child by teaching too much for extended periods of time.

_____ Teach new and complex activities at the beginning of the period when students are fresh and alert.

_____ Create classroom environment that calms down or peps up the child (as appropriate).

_____ Keep expectations at a realistic level; do not expect child to sit too long.

_____ Be aware that it may take so much cognitive and emotional energy to sit still, that the child may not have enough energy available for learning. Therefore, allow a certain amount of fidgeting.

_____ Provide the majority of the instruction on a one-to-one basis or in a small group.

_____ Provide immediate reinforcement for desired behavior; e.g., award ribbons or certificates to encourage participation.

_____ Keep activities varied but structured; always work toward a goal that the students know.

_____ Increase the attention span by providing short concentrated work periods with a gradual increase in working time.

_____ Set up the class according to a routine or orderly procedure. If students know what is coming next, they are more secure.

_____ Have a prompt and consistent approach to starting work.

_____ Help students remember better by using visual aids.

_____ Make students feel secure. Experiences must not be threatening.

_____ Remove distracting objects.

_____ Do not strive for control at all times; allow free-play periods.

_____ Follow programs that stress the development of social competency and personal adequacy.

_____ Work on specific parts of the skill before demonstrating and teaching the entire skill.

_____ Make the explanations concise and brief.

_____ Be aware of the language understanding level of the child when giving verbal instructions.

_____ Emphasize vocal and motor "output modalities" that are generated during activities; for example, have the child describe what he is doing as he is stimulated to move through the environment

_____ Make all commands short, direct, and simple. Expect a response after the command; give the child time to think it through.

_____ Provide a "quiet area" in which children can work.

_____ Give instructions orally in a clear, well-modulated voice.

_____ Have the child repeat instructions before she performs to reinforce auditory clues.

_____ Provide frequent breaks in seatwork with chance to move around the room.

_____ Use masking tape or carpet square to mark the child's space.

_____ Change the activity before students become bored.

Case Study

Matt is a young boy attending kindergarten at his neighborhood school. During the first few months of the year, his teacher has noted that Matt has demonstrated excessive restlessness throughout the school day. Often his teacher has observed that he constantly needs to move throughout the classroom, fidgets excessively when he is sitting, appears not to attend to classroom instruction, and cannot keep up with the class routine, apparently due to the excessive restlessness. The classroom teacher filled out a Pre-Referral Motor Screening Checklist and the consultation process began. The adapted physical education (A.P.E.) specialist, occupational and physical therapists were called in to observe Matt in the classroom and other settings throughout the day. Each specialist found concerns similar to the classroom teacher's and agreed with the original findings. After discussion, the following general recommendations were made for the teacher to implement strategies for Matt:

1) Provide Matt with a desk in both the front and back of the room so he can move between class activities.
2) Allow Matt to choose alternate positions when working: on his stomach on the floor, sitting in a beanbag chair, or sitting backwards in his chair so that his legs straddle the seat and his chest is against the back of the chair.
3) Use short, concentrated work periods with gradual increases in working time as Matt can tolerate.
4) Do not strive for control at all time; allow Matt free-play periods throughout the day.
5) Keep expectations at a realistic level; do not expect Matt to sit for extended periods of time.
6) Remove distracting objects in Matt's visual field near his desk as well as the classroom.

The classroom teacher began implementing these general considerations. The classroom environment became less distracting for Matt, the pace of instruction was altered to "fit" Matt more appropriately, and the teacher reached a more realistic approach and expectation level.

The following specific activities/recommendations were suggested by the specialists for Matt to engage in strategies that would enhance his abilities to deal with his excessive restlessness:

1) Provide a "quiet area" in which Matt can work.

2) Have Matt manipulate small objects (squishy balls, balloon filled with flour, etc.) while listening to class instructions.

3) Have Matt help move chairs and/or desks throughout the day, beginning with lighter objects and moving to heavier ones.

4) Before beginning an activity that will require Matt to sit for an extended period of time, he and his classmates can bend, stretch, twist, turn, and shake body parts using creative drama or to music.

5) Provide a bungee cord/therapy band around the front two legs of his chair so Matt can push against it throughout the day. If using the second desk and chair, have the same set-up for both desks.

6) Allow Matt to sit on a T-stool as needed throughout the day. The vestibular input needed can be provided by the use of this stool.

7) Matt can wear earplugs while working at his desk to eliminate external noises that may distract him.

Using these specific strategies as well as the general considerations, the teacher has intervened in a nonthreatening manner and has provided opportunities for Matt to engage in activities specifically for his needs. It was recommended to follow-up in six to eight weeks to observe and note if changes have been made in Matt's profile. The specialists re-checked with the teacher and observed again in the classroom and other settings throughout the day. Progress had been made. More discussion was made and a few more strategies were introduced as Matt continued to improve his ability to participate in classroom activities. As recommended by the specialists, the teacher met with the parents and provided similar ideas for home use. Consistent and concrete structure at home and school will only enhance Matt's abilities.

Progress continued; however, Matt's teacher noted that when Matt needed to sit at his desk he often would shift his body constantly, lean on the desk, often sit up on the front edge of the chair, even falling out of the chair at times. The teacher notified the Motor team (adapted physical education specialist, physical therapist, and occupational therapist) for further assistance on this issue. The adapted physical education specialist came to the classroom and specifically observed Matt working at his desk. All of the concerns the teacher noted were observed by this specialist as well. What appeared at first to be part of Matt's distractibility turned out to be a problem with Matt's chair and desk; they were not designed at the proper heights. Matt's chair was too small for the desk. After more than one observation, the specialist determined that the chair height needed to be increased. In this case the chair could not be adjusted. Another chair from a higher grade was brought in and fit appropriately to the desk height. Matt was able to sit at his desk with his feet equally placed on the ground, in an upright posture that did not make him reach up or down to write on the desk. The height of the desk was 2 inches (5 cm) above Matt's flexed elbows (at 90 degrees) when seated.

Matt was observed constantly moving at his original desk simply because he was constantly trying to find a comfortable position in which to work. He was shifting his body weight and engaging muscles that were not necessary. Therefore, he fatigued these muscle groups and needed to move to another position to "rest" those muscles, in turn engaging new muscle groups. This pattern continued throughout the day as Matt was required to sit and work at his desk. Another observation was made that the teacher did not even observe: that Matt stood at his desk often to work. It was his way of relaxing muscle groups, using the skeleton to bear weight relaxing most muscle groups.

The best posture for writing is sitting with the hips against the back of the chair, knees bent at 90 degrees, and feet flat on the floor. Because of the smaller chair, Matt was not able to sit with his hips against the back of the chair. If he tried, he was not able to reach forward and place his arms and hands on the desk height. His knees were never bent at 90 degrees. When his teacher asked him to sit "correctly" in his chair his knees were bent in the 60-70 degree range. His feet were on the ground but not always stationary. He would often need to move his feet to find more comfortable positions. As we can see Matt needed a simple change in his chair and/or desk height.

After the initial consultation and suggested strategies, Matt made some progress. But it was the second set of observations and findings that provided the most important changes in Matt's program; his chair and desk orientation. Now the teacher has reported that Matt tolerates much longer periods of time doing his deskwork. The quality of his writing and fine motor activities has also improved. The most impressive finding of all in this situation turned out that the teacher, now much more aware of the "children," not the "curriculum," has adjusted all the desks and chairs for all of her students!

Fine Motor Problems

If One or More of These Characteristics Are Exhibited . . .

- ☐ Has difficulty manipulating small objects (pegs, beads, coins)
- ☐ Has difficulty using scissors, coloring, and writing
- ☐ Abnormal pencil grip (holds tightly or weakly; immature grasp)
- ☐ Jerky or tremor-like motions in hands when drawing
- ☐ Has difficulty staying on lines when tracing
- ☐ Eyes do not follow hands or seem to wander
- ☐ Has difficulty using isolated finger movements (uses arm and hand as one unit)

Try These Activities

(Some activities incorporate more than one sensory-motor skill and are listed under the appropriate categories.)

Vestibular

_____ Adjust chair height so child's feet can be placed flat on floor and knees are at 90-degree angle.

_____ Have children move in different directions and in various ways to develop dynamic and static balance.

Tactile

_____ Use a rubber pencil grip.

_____ Draw shapes or zigzag lines on a carpet sample. Have the child erase the marks using her hands or fingers.

_____ At the blackboard, have the child use tiny pieces of chalk to write words and draw pictures.

_____ Draw letters, zigzag lines, or repeated shapes in flattened clay, sand, finger paint, or shaving cream with finger.

_____ Use a vibrating pen for "fun writing."

_____ Form letters with chenille stems or clay.

_____ Squeeze small balloons filled with flour.

_____ Pop bubble wrap.

_____ Rip construction paper scraps for art projects.

_____ Connect the holes in lacing pictures by threading shoe laces from one hole to another. (Also Motor Planning)

_____ Have the child chew chewy candy, gum, rubber tubing, etc.

Motor Planning

_____ Complete puzzles with small, interlocking pieces.

_____ Perform fingerplays before writing sessions.

_____ Draw letters in flattened clay with a pencil or chopsticks.

_____ Form letters with chenille stems or clay.

_____ Learn finger snapping.

_____ Pick up small items with tweezers, starting with cotton and progressing to pebbles.

_____ Use eyedroppers to transfer colored water into small containers.

_____ Have child attach spring-form clothespins to items.

_____ Play made-up games using tongs/basters.

_____ Place small items in jars with lids so child has to screw the lids off and on.

_____ Have children move their heads, shoulders, arms, hands, or trunks while sitting or lying.

_____ Encourage the children to bend, stretch, twist, turn, and shake as many parts of their bodies as possible while standing, sitting, or lying.

_____ To improve hand and finger manipulation (also Bilateral Motor Coordination):

> ▶ Get a coin out a purse one at a time, hiding in hand.
> ▶ Crumple paper.
> ▶ Take lid off a jar and hold it in palm while getting objects out of jar.
> ▶ Put coins into a bank one at a time.
> ▶ String beads and pieces of straws.
> ▶ Rub paint or glue off finger with finger of same hand.
> ▶ Screw nuts and bolts together.
> ▶ Form clay into balls with fingertips.
> ▶ Pin clothes pins onto a clothes line.
> ▶ Drop color onto paper with eyedropper.
> ▶ Flip coins.
> ▶ Spin tops.
> ▶ Move a marble across, up, and down a wall with thumb, middle, and index and finger.

_____ Correlate physical education activities with classroom activities to provide reinforcement of academic concepts, such as "Alphabet Relay." This simple relay game incorporates gross motor development skills (locomotor skills) and academic concepts. The children can be divided into four to five groups sitting on the floor in a line on one side of the classroom, gym, or playing area. On the opposite side of the area are piles of laminated alphabet letters placed in front of each line. On command, the first child of each line performs a locomotor skill (hops) to the pile of mixed-up letters, finds the "A," and returns performing the same locomotor skill. The second child continues and finds the "B." The process continues until the first group completes the task of stacking the alphabet. The second child in turn then moves to find the "B" and places it on top of the "A". This continues until all letters are placed in order. The first group to complete the task is the "winner." The objectives of this game are group cooperation and participation, language arts/cognitive development, recognition of letters, sequencing, and locomotor skill development.

Bilateral Motor Coordination

____ Remind child to stabilize paper with her nondominant hand.
____ Have the child work at the blackboard, on a wall, or at an easel.
____ At the blackboard, use tiny pieces of chalk.
____ Perform action rhyme stories before writing sessions.
____ Erase or wash chalkboards.
____ Have the child cut materials such as clay, straws, sandpaper, oak tag, felt, etc.
____ Use a stapler and hole puncher on sheets of scrap paper.
____ Encourage the child to wear weighted mitts intermittently during writing exercises (under supervision from the therapist).
____ Have the child secure papers together using spring-loaded paper clips.
____ Pull pieces of masking tape off wall.
____ Have the child squeeze/pinch clay prior to writing activity.
____ Rip paper for art projects. (Also Proprioceptive/Kinesthetic)
____ Shuffle a deck of cards.
____ Crumple paper and stuff art projects.
(Also Proprioceptive/Kinesthetic)
____ Squeeze soft balls.
____ Play made-up games using tongs/basters to move game pieces.
____ Store small items in jars with lids so child has to screw the lids off and on.

Proprioceptive/Kinesthetic

____ Use resistive activities; for example, pull back on the child's arm as she tries to bring it forward
____ Do finger exercises before writing activities; e.g., shake out hands and rub hands together.

_____ Have the child squeeze/pinch clay prior to writing activity.

_____ Use a vibrating pen for "fun writing."

_____ Have the child deliver books to the library.

_____ For the seal walk, have the child start in the prone position on the floor with weight on hands and toes and pull himself forward.

_____ Practice the wheelbarrow walk by walking on hands while the feet are held off the floor by a partner.

_____ Have the child spread fingers far apart and then bring them together and make a tight fist.

_____ Encourage the child to place spring-type clothespins around the edge of a shoe box.

_____ Allow the child to choose alternate positions for working; e.g., on stomach on floor, curled up in corner, etc.

_____ Have the child wear a heavy backpack.

_____ Have the child press palms together.

_____ Provide proprioceptive activities prior to fine motor activities (e.g., pushing, pulling, and squeezing).

_____ Crumple paper and stuff art projects.

_____ Squeeze soft balls.

_____ Have the child perform fingerplays and hand rhymes before a writing session.

_____ Use maximum stimuli such as the following in teaching new skills:
- ▶ Kinesthetic stimuli: guiding of body parts through desired movement for a physical sense or feeling of the pattern
- ▶ Tactile stimuli: use touch to relate more effectively to the child which part of the body is to be used; also the child may learn more about equipment and environment by touch
- ▶ Visual stimuli: use visual aids such as slides, diagrams, demonstrations, pictures, films, and mirrors (be alert that mirrors may confuse right and left concepts)
- ▶ Verbal stimuli: give oral instructions as the child performs

_____ Use activities in which the child must identify his body parts, move them, and be aware of their positions in space.

_____ Let students put their hands on your shoulders or hips or be led physically so they receive the kinesthetic feeling of the following concepts:
- ▶ Time—show fast, slow, or uneven time by running or walking with the students.
- ▶ Space—lead the students around so they understand distances and the area of the classroom.
- ▶ Size—physically show the students how to be tall, short, or wide, and relate this to their environment.

_____ Have children move their arms and hands frequently while sitting or lying.

_____ Encourage the children to bend, stretch, twist, turn, and shake arms and shoulders while standing, sitting, or lying.

Equilibrium

_____ Adjust the chair height so child's feet are flat on floor and knees are at 90-degree angle when sitting on the chair.

_____ Allow the child to use other positions; e.g., standing, kneeling, laying on her belly on the floor, etc., for stability.

_____ Practice jumping jacks.

_____ Have the child deliver books to the library.

_____ Have the child sit in a chair backwards so that the legs straddle the seat and the chest is against the back of the chair.

_____ Have children move in different directions and in various ways to develop dynamic and static balance.

General Suggestions

_____ Adjust desk height so the writing surface reaches 2" (5 cm) above the child's bent elbow.

_____ Adjust paper to a 40-degree angle.

_____ Use a multisensory approach to teaching.

_____ Structure activities from the least difficult and well-known concepts to the most difficult and unknown, since success is of prime importance.

_____ Use a variety of auditory, tactile, visual, and proprioceptive modes in isolation and in combination.

_____ Tape paper to desk to remind child to slant paper.

_____ Remind child to stabilize paper with his nondominant hand.

_____ Have the child use a pencil length no less than 5" (13 cm).

_____ Provide well-sharpened pencils.

_____ Take off "do dads" from the ends of pencils.

_____ Use a primary red pencil.

_____ Allow the child to use a felt-tip pen at times.

_____ Have the child work on a vertical surface; e.g., whiteboard and easel.

_____ Thicken the lines for tracing.

_____ Proceed with motor development from gross to fine movements and from movement of the trunk to movement of the extremities.

Seems Excessively Distracted by Stimulation

If One or More of These Characteristics Are Exhibited . . .

- ❑ Dislikes light touch or being touched
- ❑ Overreacts to unexpected touch or sound
- ❑ Unable to calm down after motor activity
- ❑ Avoids getting messy in glue, sand, finger paint, or tape
- ❑ Displays unusual need for touching certain toys, surfaces, or textures
- ❑ Has decreased awareness of pain or temperature
- ❑ Other: _____

Try These Activities

(Some activities incorporate more than one sensory-motor skill and are listed under the appropriate categories.)

Vestibular

_____ Allow the child to stand while working on tasks.

_____ Have children bend, stretch, twist, turn, and shake as many parts of the body as possible while standing, sitting, or lying.

Tactile

_____ Have the tactile-defensive child stand at end of the line of children.

_____ Whenever touching the child, make sure the appropriate touch is deep and firm.

_____ Provide large bolts and nuts for the child to manipulate. Have the child screw the nut all the way on the bolt.

_____ Squeeze/pinch clay prior to writing activity.

_____ Hide objects in rice, sand, or styrene-foam packing material in the tactile bin. Have the child dig in the bin to find the objects.

_____ Make special lacing pictures by gluing various fabric textures on the art, then use a hole puncher to make the holes. Have the child thread a shoe lace through the holes and feel the fabric pieces.

_____ Trace sandpaper letters with index finger.

_____ Trace letter shapes on carpet samples with index finger.

_____ Form letters with chenille stems or clay.

_____ To improve tactile awareness, encourage the child to work with crazy foam, shaving cream, whipping cream, pudding, finger paints, and/or hand lotion.

____   To improve tactile discrimination:
- ► Play finger games/songs.
- ► Play the guessing game "What do you feel?" (discriminate textures, shapes, objects).
- ► Try crawling or rolling on textures without looking and guess what they are.
- ► Write or draw shapes, numbers, and letters with your finger on the child's body and ask him to identify them.

Motor Planning

____   Have the child draw letters in flattened clay with a pencil or chopsticks.

____   Have the children do "mystery writing" while at chalkboard with their eyes closed. Guide their hands to write letters or words and then have them guess what they wrote.

Bilateral Motor Coordination

____   Trace letters on carpet samples with index finger.

____   Form letters with chenille stems or clay.

Proprioceptive/Kinesthetic

_____ Have the child assist with moving classroom furniture. Try smaller items first and progress to larger and heavier ones, as the child seems able. (Also Tactile)

_____ Have the child jump on a mini-trampoline.

_____ Encourage the child to squeeze small rubber balls.

_____ Have the child crumple a small piece of paper into a small ball with one hand.

_____ Allow the child to choose alternate positions for working, e.g., on stomach on floor, curled up in corner, etc.

_____ Suggest that the child wear tight-fitting clothing; e.g., tights, spandex, suspenders, or weighted vest.

_____ Place sandbags, beanbags, or bolsters on child's lap at appropriate times.

_____ Have the child wear heavy backpack.

_____ Have the child sit on hands.

_____ Provide proprioceptive activities; e.g., pushing, pulling, and squeezing, prior to fine motor activities.

_____ Incorporate deep pressure exercises into daily routine:

- ► shifting weight in sitting from side to side
- ► pressing hands together
- ► putting hands on top of head and pressing down
- ► crossing arms and press on shoulders with opposite hand
- ► putting hands on knees and pressing down
- ► putting hands under opposite elbows and press up
- ► rotating shoulders and then upper trunk side to side
- ► tilting head rhythmically side to side
- ► brushing hands down arms firmly

_____ Whenever touching the child, make sure that the touch is deep and firm.

____ Use maximum stimuli such as the following in teaching new skills:

- ► Kinesthetic stimuli: guide the child's body parts through desired movement for a physical sense of the pattern.
- ► Tactile stimuli: use touch to relate more effectively to the child which part of the body is to be used; also, the child may learn more about the equipment and environment by touch.
- ► Visual stimuli: use visual aids such as slides, diagrams, demonstrations, pictures, films, and mirrors. Be aware that mirrors may confuse understanding of right and left concepts.
- ► Verbal stimuli: give oral instructions as the child performs.

____ Let students put their hands on your shoulders or hips or be led physically so they receive the kinesthetic feeling of the following concepts:

- ► Time—show fast, slow, or uneven time by running or walking with the students.
- ► Space—lead the student around so he understands distances and the area of the classroom.
- ► Size—physically show the students how to be tall, short, or wide, and relate this to their environment.

____ Have students push and pull using elbows, arms, hands, and trunks while lying, sitting, or standing.

Equilibrium

____ Have the child sit in chair backwards so that the legs straddle the seat and the chest is against the back of the chair.

____ Allow the child to stand while working on tasks.

____ Have the children move in different directions and in various ways to develop dynamic and static balance.

____ Have the children bend, stretch, twist, turn, and shake as many parts of their bodies as possible while standing, sitting, or lying.

General Suggestions

_____ Keep expectations at a realistic level; do not expect children to sit too long.

_____ Give the child a desk at both the front and back of the room so she can move between class activities.

_____ Give short and simple instructions.

_____ Teach new and complex activities at the beginning of the period when students are fresh.

_____ Work on specific parts of the skill before demonstrating and teaching the entire skill.

_____ Do not cover too much in one session.

_____ Change the activity before students become bored.

_____ Allow the children enough room to have some freedom of movement but make the area confining enough to maintain order and interest in the activity.

_____ Be gentle but firm. Some students may be timid or lack confidence and others may be rather aggressive. A comfortable learning situation needs to be present for both.

_____ Read facial expressions and body gestures to anticipate the future.

_____ Create a classroom environment that calms down or peps up the child (as appropriate).

_____ Provide frequent breaks when doing deskwork, giving the child an opportunity to move around the room.

_____ Establish eye contact when giving instruction to students.

_____ Be in full view of all children when giving explanations.

_____ Stand still and be in a place in the room where shadows are least likely to be on the face.

_____ Make explanations concise and brief.

_____ Begin teaching where the student is functioning.

_____ Structure activities from the least difficult and known concepts to the most difficult and unknown since success is of prime importance.

_____ Help increase the attention span of children by providing short, concentrated work periods with a gradual increase in working time.

_____ Give the child one task at a time to perform.

_____ Use activities in which the child must identify his body parts, move them, and be aware of their position in space.

_____ Do not strive for control at all times. Allow free-play periods.

Trouble with Attention

If One or More of These Characteristics Are Exhibited . . .

❏ Is lethargic at times
❏ Stares blankly on occasion
❏ Frequently misses directions
❏ Has wandering eyes; cannot focus
❏ Avoids eye contact
❏ Does not notice when people come into the room
❏ Jumps from one activity to another frequently and thus interferes with own play
❏ Other: _____

Try These Activities

(Some activities incorporate more than one sensory/motor skill and are listed under the appropriate categories.)

Vestibular

_____ Child should be able to sit upright in chair while still having feet flat on floor.

_____ Have children move in different directions and in various ways to develop dynamic and static balance. (Also Equilibrium)

_____ Provide the child with a variety of spinning activities immediately before you want the maximum amount of attentiveness to occur. Examples include: spinning in an office chair three times to the right and then three times to the left, for about ten times total; rolling on carpet or floor mat; spinning on a scooter board; etc.

Tactile

_____ Allow the child to play with toys in water table or large plastic bucket filled with water. Be sure to have the child dry herself with a cloth towel.

_____ Provide opportunities for the child to prepare simple food dishes or work with bread dough.

_____ Squeeze/pinch clay prior to a writing activity.

_____ Suggest that child wear tight-fitting clothing; e.g., tights, spandex, suspenders, or weighted vest.

_____ Provide tactile bin in classroom for "down time."

_____ Trace sandpaper or carpet sample letters with index finger.

____ Add sand to finger paint and have child draw letters in it.

____ Use a variety of tactile mediums to reinforce what you are teaching the child visually. Examples include: have the child write letters and numbers in cornmeal; write letters and numbers on the child's back and have the child reproduce them on paper; provide the opportunity for forming letters and numbers without vision to help internalize the movements required and to help increase the child's kinesthetic awareness.

Motor Planning

____ Provide activities to improve spatial awareness, laterality, directionality, body image, skillful movement performances, postural maintenance, and locating of sounds or objects.

____ Draw letters in flattened clay with a pencil or chopsticks.

____ Have the children do "mystery writing" at chalkboard with their eyes closed. Guide their hands to write letters or words and then have them guess what they wrote.

____ Have children move their heads, shoulders, arms, hands, or trunks while sitting or lying.

____ Encourage the children to bend, stretch, twist, turn, and shake as many parts of their bodies as possible while standing, sitting, or lying down.

Bilateral Motor Coordination

____ Erase or wash chalkboards.

____ Squeeze or pinch clay prior to writing activity.

Proprioceptive/Kinesthetic

____ Have the child assist with moving classroom furniture. Try smaller items first and progress to larger and heavier ones, as the child seems able. (Also Tactile)

____ Squeeze/pinch clay prior to writing activity.

____ Have the child sit in chair backwards so that the legs straddle the seat and the chest is against the back of the chair.

____ Allow child to choose alternate positions for working; e.g., on stomach on floor, curled up in corner, etc.

____ Use resistive activities; e.g., pull back on the child's arm as she tries to bring it forward.

____ Have the child sit on hands.

____ Place sandbags, beanbags, or bolsters on child's lap at appropriate times.

____ Incorporate deep pressure exercises into daily routine:
- ► shifting weight in sitting from side to side
- ► pressing hands together
- ► putting hands on top of head and pressing down
- ► crossing arms and press on shoulders with opposite hand
- ► putting hands on knees and pressing down
- ► putting hands under opposite elbows and press up
- ► rotating shoulders and then upper trunk side to side
- ► tilting head rhythmically side to side
- ► brushing hands down arms firmly

____ Use maximum stimuli such as the following in teaching new skills:
- ► Kinesthetic stimuli: guide the child's body parts through desired movement for a physical sense of the pattern.
- ► Tactile stimuli: use touch to relate more effectively to the child which part of the body is to be used; also, the child may learn more about the equipment and environment by touch.
- ► Visual stimuli: use visual aids such as slides, diagrams, demonstrations, pictures, films, and mirrors. Be aware that mirrors may confuse understanding of right and left concepts.
- ► Verbal stimuli: give oral instructions as the child performs.

____ Let students put their hands on your shoulders or hips or be led physically so they receive the kinesthetic feeling of the following concepts:
- ► Time—show fast, slow, or uneven time by running or walking with the students.
- ► Space—lead the students around so they understand distances and the area of the classroom.
- ► Size—physically show the students how to be tall, short, or wide, and relate this to their environment.

____ Provide a variety of firm-pressure touches immediately before you want the maximum amount of attention to occur. Examples include: roll back and forth on a rug surface, do caterpillar activity, try rubbing warm-ups where the child firmly rubs his own shoulders, arms, and hands with a dry washcloth, roll a ball up and down a child's back while he tells you where to roll the ball, and so forth.

____ Have student push and pull using elbows, arms, hands, and trunk while lying, sitting, or standing.

____ Allow the child to play barefoot. Receptors on the soles of the feet signal changes in texture and weight.

Equilibrium

____ Have the child sit in chair backwards so that the legs straddle the seat and the chest is against the back of the chair. (Also Tactile, Proprioceptive/Kinesthetic)

____ Child should be able to sit upright in chair while still having feet flat on floor.

____ Have the child sit on T-stool or therapy ball.

General Suggestions

____ Use proper lighting in rooms to avoid shadows and other visual illusions.

____ Turn off fluorescent lights.

____ Keep expectations at a realistic level; do not expect children to sit too long.

____ Give short and simple instructions.

____ Make explanations concise and brief.

_____ Establish eye contact when giving instructions to students.

_____ Be in full view of all children when giving explanations.

_____ Give instructions orally in a clear, well-modulated voice.

_____ Be sure to have the child's attention as you start to give instructions.

_____ Provide "quiet area" for child to work in.

_____ Create a classroom environment that calms down or peps up the child (as appropriate).

_____ Provide child with earplugs/headphones.

_____ Begin teaching where the student is functioning.

_____ Give the child one task at a time to perform.

_____ Avoid doing a task the same way each time, since this makes the child learn isolated skills.

_____ Provide opportunities for children to work in environments with a low level of extraneous stimulation; e.g., cubbies that are quiet and have a minimum amount of visual or auditory distractions. If auditory over-stimulation is the major problem, try having the child wear a set of headphones to help block out the auditory distractions while they are being asked to attend visually.

_____ Use multisensory approach to teaching.

_____ Provide frequent breaks when doing deskwork, giving the child an opportunity to move around the room.

_____ Proceed with motor development from gross to fine movements and from movement of the trunk to movement of the extremities.

_____ If discipline is a problem, consider the possibility that the activity is too difficult to understand, requires too much skill, has too many rules, or has too many verbal instructions.

_____ Do not frustrate the child by teaching too much for extended periods of time.

_____ Teach new and complex activities at the beginning of the class period when students are fresh.

_____ Work on specific parts of a skill before demonstrating and teaching the entire skill.

_____ Change the activity before students become bored.

_____ Allow the children enough room to have some freedom of movement but make the area confining enough to maintain order and interest in the activity.

_____ Structure activities from the least difficult and known concepts to the most difficult and unknown since success is of prime importance.

_____ Keep activities varied but structured. Always work toward a goal that is known by the students.

_____ Help increase the attention span of children by providing short, concentrated work periods with a gradual increase in working time.

_____ If the child has difficulty with abstract terms, choose activities that demonstrate and relate language well to aid in the learning process.

_____ Use a variety of auditory, tactile, visual, and proprioceptive modalities in isolation and in combination to teach activities.

_____ Emphasize vocal and motor "output modalities" that are generated during activities; e.g., have the child describe what she is doing as she is stimulated to move through the environment.

_____ Be gentle but firm. Some students may be timid or lack confidence and others may be rather aggressive. A comfortable learning situation needs to be present for both.

_____ Do not be afraid to help the child through a task if he is having difficulty. Do not allow him to stop in the middle of a task and, consequently, feel frustration and failure.

_____ Make all commands short, direct, and simple. Expect a response. After the command, give the child time to think it through.

_____ Have the child repeat instructions before he performs to reinforce auditory clues.

_____ Generate auditory feedback from self-vocalization by the child and relate this meaningfully to her simultaneous motor-visual-tactile activity.

_____ Free the working area of outside distractions and noises.

_____ Alternate visual and verbal commands and signals so children learn to move to different sensory cues that may mean the same thing.

_____ Present additional stimuli as the student's attention span and listening skills improve.

_____ Emphasize activities that develop the awareness of sensory input of touch, smell, taste, hearing, and proprioception.

_____ Encourage students to give ideas and steer responses to types of movement suggested by activities in the story.

_____ Have the child act out incidents he has experienced or heard to incorporate motor planning skills.

_____ Provide kinesthetic cues, which may range from a signal, such as a tap on the shoulder, to actually leading the child through the movement.

Learning Behavior

If One or More of These Characteristics Are Exhibited . . .

- ❑ Short attention span
- ❑ Difficulty with change in routine
- ❑ Difficulty recognizing own errors
- ❑ Difficulty working independently
- ❑ Slow worker
- ❑ Easily distracted
- ❑ Perseverate
- ❑ Disorganized, messy
- ❑ Talks aloud, hums, sings

Try These Activities

(Some activities incorporate more than one sensory/motor skill and are listed under the appropriate categories.)

Tactile

_____ Hide objects in rice, sand, or styrene-foam packing material in the tactile bin. Have the child dig in the bin to find the objects.

_____ Make lacing pictures by gluing various fabric textures on poster board, then use a hole puncher to make the holes. Have the child thread a shoe lace through the holes and feel the fabric pieces.

_____ Have the child squeeze/pinch clay prior to writing activity.

_____ Encourage the child to draw pictures in finger paints. Add sand, sawdust, and shredded paper to the paint for different textures.

_____ Trace sandpaper letters with index finger.

_____ Trace letter shapes on carpet samples with index finger.

_____ Form letters with chenille stems or clay.

_____ Have the child eat a hard, crunchy snack; e.g., apples, carrots, celery, and bagels.

_____ Have the child chew chewy candy, gum, rubber tubing, etc.

Motor Planning

_____ Have the children do "mystery writing" at chalkboard with their eyes closed. Guide their hands to write letters or words and then have them guess what they wrote.

_____ Put a picture in the bottom of the child's desk to indicate where supplies go.

_____ Place magnet clips on side of desk for organizing loose papers.

Bilateral Motor Coordination

____ Erase/wash chalkboards.

____ Squeeze/pinch clay prior to a writing activity.

____ Trace letters on carpet samples with index finger.

Proprioceptive/Kinesthetic

____ Have the child assist with moving classroom furniture. Try smaller items first and progress to larger and heavier ones, as the child seems able. (Also Tactile)

____ Play games with small pieces, such as checkers, or marbles.

____ Have the child sit in chair backwards so that the legs straddle the seat and the chest is against the back of the chair.

____ Allow child to choose alternate positions for working; e.g., on stomach on floor, curled up in corner, etc.

____ Have the child sit on hands.

____ Place sandbags, beanbags, or bolsters on child's lap.

____ Incorporate deep pressure exercises into daily routine:
- ► shifting weight in sitting from side to side
- ► pressing hands together
- ► putting hands on top of head and pressing down
- ► crossing arms and press on shoulders with opposite hands
- ► putting hands on knees and pressing down
- ► putting hands under opposite elbows and press up
- ► rotating shoulders and then upper trunk side to side
- ► tilting head rhythmically side to side
- ► brushing hands down arms firmly

____ Use maximum stimuli such as the following in teaching new skills:
- ► Kinesthetic stimuli: guide the child's body parts through desired movement for a physical sense of the pattern.
- ► Tactile stimuli: use touch to relate more effectively to the child which part of the body is to be used; also, the child may learn more about the equipment and environment by touch.
- ► Visual stimuli: use visual aids, such as slides, diagrams, demonstrations, pictures, films, and mirrors. Be aware that mirrors may confuse understanding of right and left concepts.
- ► Verbal stimuli: give oral instructions as the child performs.

____ Let students put their hands on your shoulders or hips or be led physically so they receive the kinesthetic feeling of the following concepts:

> Time—show fast, slow, or uneven time by running or walking with the students.

> Space—lead the students around so they understand distances and the area of the classroom.

> Size—physically show the students how to be tall, short, or wide, and relate this to their environment.

____ Provide deep-pressure touch to hyperactive/distractible child periodically throughout the day.

____ Have the child chew chewy candy, gum, rubber tubing, etc.

Equilibrium

____ Have the child sit in chair backwards so that the legs straddle the seat and the chest is against the back of the chair. (Also Tactile)

General Suggestions

____ Give short and simple instructions.

____ Provide a "quiet area" for child to work in.

____ If discipline is a problem, consider the possibility that the activity is too difficult to understand, requires too much skill, has too many rules, or has too many verbal instructions.

____ Do not frustrate the child by teaching too much for extended periods of time.

____ Teach new and complex activities at the beginning of the class period when students are fresh and alert.

____ Create a classroom environment that calms down or peps up the child (as appropriate).

____ Provide child with earplugs/headphones.

____ Have the child use graph paper to help guide spatial placement.

____ Use masking tape or carpet square to mark child's space.

____ Use color-coded file folders to organize papers.

_____ Have the child use a book shelf for storage, instead of a desk—or have a box on the floor.

_____ Have the child routinely organize desk.

_____ Put a picture in the bottom of the child's desk, indicating where supplies go.

_____ Place magnet clips on side of desk for loose papers.

_____ Give the child a list of the scheduled activities or use a flip-card system at the child's desk.

_____ Work on parts of a skill before demonstrating and teaching the entire skill.

_____ Keep explanations concise and brief.

_____ Do not cover too much in one session.

_____ Change the activity before students become bored.

_____ Allow children enough room to have some freedom of movement but make the area confining enough to maintain order and interest in the activity.

_____ Establish eye contact when giving instruction to students.

_____ Be in full view of all children when giving explanations.

_____ Allow the child to practice and repeat skills for the pleasure of doing something successfully.

_____ Begin teaching where the student is functioning.

_____ Structure activities from the least difficult and known concept to the most difficult and unknown since success is of prime importance.

_____ Keep activities varied but structured; always work toward a goal that is known by the students.

_____ Help increase the attention span of children by providing short, concentrated work periods with a gradual increase in working time.

_____ Since the child may have difficulty with abstract terms, activities that demonstrate and relate language will aid in the learning process.

_____ Use a variety of auditory, tactile, visual, and proprioceptive modalities in isolation and in combination to teach activities.

_____ Be gentle but firm. Some students may be timid or lack confidence and others may be rather aggressive. A comfortable learning situation needs to be present for both.

_____ Make all commands short, direct, and simple. Expect a response. After the command, give the child time to think it through.

_____ Light rooms properly to avoid shadows and other visual illusions.

_____ Give instructions orally in a clear, well-modulated voice.

_____ Have the child repeat instructions before he performs to reinforce auditory clues.

_____ Free the working area of outside distractions and noises.

_____ Give the child one task at a time to perform.

_____ Use activities in which the child must identify her body parts, move them, and be aware of their positions in space.

_____ Encourage the child to watch your face when you are talking to the group.

_____ When speaking, try to face the student as much as possible.

_____ Give important instructions from a position close to the child.

_____ Stand still and be in a place in the room where shadows are least likely to be on the face.

_____ When giving oral directions, choose one place to stand and do not walk around while talking. Try to come back to this place if more instruction must be given after the activity has begun.

_____ Be sure to have the child's attention as you start to give instructions.

_____ Provide kinesthetic cues, which may range from a signal, such as a tap on the shoulder, to actually leading the child through the movement.

_____ Provide immediate reinforcement for desired behavior; awarding ribbons or certificates stimulates participation.

_____ Set up the class according to a routine or orderly procedure. If students know what is coming next, they feel more secure.

_____ Have a prompt and consistent approach to starting work.

_____ Help students remember better by using visual aids.

_____ Make students feel secure; experiences must not be threatening.

_____ Increase the attention span of students by removing distracting objects.

Weakness or Floppiness of Arms and Legs

If One or More of These Characteristics Are Exhibited . . .

- ❑ Cannot easily get up from the floor or a chair
- ❑ Trouble going up or down stairs
- ❑ Appears to fatigue easily
- ❑ Seems weaker or stronger than normal
- ❑ Tires easily; has poor endurance
- ❑ Cannot lift heavy objects

Try These Activities

(Some activities incorporate more than one sensory/motor skill and are listed under the appropriate categories.)

Vestibular

_____ Have the child move through classroom in novel ways; e.g., walking backwards/sideways, hopping, crawling, etc. (Also Motor Planning)

_____ Child lies on his side on the floor, head resting on arm extended under him, top hand on floor at chest. Keeping the body in a straight line, he lifts both legs from the floor as high as possible.

_____ Encourage the child to stand with arms and legs crossed and then sit down and rise to standing at once.

_____ Standing on mat with arms extended at sides for balance, the child lifts one leg in front of her with knee straight and then bends knee of supporting leg, squats low, and returns at once to standing position.

Tactile

_____ Have the child play catch at close range with a partner by tossing a medicine ball back and forth.

_____ Use vibrating pen for "fun writing."

_____ Have the child chew chewy candy, gum, rubber tubing, etc.

Motor Planning

_____ Have the children do "mystery writing" at chalkboard with eyes closed. Guide their hands to write letters or words and then have them guess what they wrote.

_____ Have the child walk like different animals; e.g., crab, bear, ostrich, frog, inchworm. (Also Bilateral Motor Coordination)

_____ Play hopscotch.

 0-7424-0268-1 • Sensory Integration

Bilateral Motor Coordination

____ Erase/wash chalkboards.

____ Squeeze/pinch clay prior to writing activity.

____ Have the child cut materials such as clay, straws, sandpaper, felt.

____ Use a stapler or hole puncher on sheets of scrap paper.

____ Have the child secure papers together using spring-loaded paper clips.

Proprioceptive/Kinesthetic

____ Have student sit facing a partner, holding hands and feet in contact with legs extended. One student leans forward and the other student leans back, then reverse roles for rowboat action.

____ Practice making circles with arms while holding dumbbells.

____ Have the child assist with moving classroom furniture. Try smaller items first and progress to larger and heavier ones, as child seems able. (Also Tactile)

____ Wrap bungee cord/therapy band around front two legs of chair so that child can push against it with her legs.

____ Weight down school supplies such as pencil boxes, notebooks, etc., with washers or plaster of Paris.

____ Suggest that child wear tight-fitting clothing; e.g., tights, spandex, suspenders, or weighted vest. (Also Tactile)

____ Have the child wear a heavy backpack.

____ Allow the child to jump on a mini-trampoline.

____ Place sandbags, bean bags, or bolsters on child's lap at appropriate times.

_____ Use maximum stimuli such as the following in teaching new skills:

Kinesthetic stimuli: guide the child's body parts through desired movement for a physical sense of the pattern.

Tactile stimuli: use touch to relate more effectively to the child which part of the body is to be used; also, the child may learn more about the equipment and environment by touch.

Visual stimuli: use visual aids such as slides, diagrams, demonstrations, pictures, films, and mirrors. Be aware that mirrors may confuse understanding of right and left concepts.

Verbal stimuli: give oral instructions as the child performs.

_____ Let students put their hands on your shoulders or hips or be led physically so they receive the kinesthetic feeling of the following concepts:

Time—show fast, slow, or uneven time by running or walking with the students.

Space—lead the student around so she understands distances and the area of the classroom.

Size—physically show the students how to be tall, short, or wide, and relate this to their environment.

_____ Use resistive activities. For example, pull back on the child's arm as he tries to bring it forward.

_____ Have children move their heads, shoulders, arms, hands, or trunks while sitting or lying.

_____ Encourage the children to bend, stretch, twist, turn, and shake as many parts of their bodies as possible while standing, sitting, or lying. (Also Vestibular, Motor Planning)

Equilibrium

_____ Have the child sit in chair backwards so that the legs straddle the seat and the chest is against the back of the chair.

_____ Have the child run several steps and then leap in a forward direction, landing lightly, and moving alone.

_____ Child squats, arms folded across her chest. From this position, keeping the knees bent, she jumps forward several times.

_____ Encourage the children to move in different directions and in various ways to develop dynamic and static balance.

General Suggestions

_____ Use multisensory approach to teaching.

_____ Create classroom environment that calms down or peps up the child (as appropriate).

_____ Provide proprioceptive activities; e.g., pushing, pulling, and squeezing, prior to fine motor activities.

_____ Proceed with motor development from gross to fine movements and from movement of the trunk to movement of the extremities.

_____ Allow children enough room to have some freedom of movement but make the area confining enough to maintain order and interest in the activity.

_____ Encourage children to work and move in space to be aware of their relationship to others and their environment.

_____ Provide the child with experiences in manipulating his environment.

_____ Keep the environment simple and free from outside noises and distractions.

_____ Provide kinesthetic cues, which may range from a signal, such as a tap on the shoulder, to actually leading the child through the movement.

Case Study

Patti is in third grade and her teacher comments that she appears to tire easily, has poor endurance, appears to fatigue easily, and has trouble going up or down stairs. Her classroom is on the second level of her school and all her special classes (art, music, and P.E.) are all downstairs. The auditorium, cafeteria, and outside activities are all on the first level. Due to Patti's apparent low muscular tone and endurance, she has fallen behind in her classroom activities. When she writes with her pencils, all of her words are written with very little pressure. Patti's teacher is very concerned about her difficulties because Patti appears to be a bright child. After filling out the Pre-referral Motor Screening Checklist, the adapted physical education (A.P.E.) specialist and the physical therapist observed Patti in her classroom activities, while ascending and descending stairs, in P.E. class, and at recess activities. In each setting, the specialists observed Patti having difficulty with maintaining levels of endurance and strength as she engaged in activities. She struggled keeping up in P.E. class and was very sedentary at recess. In the classroom, she often had her head on her desk or was slouched in her seat. The following general recommendations were made for the teacher:

1) Keep expectations at a realistic level; do not expect Patti to sit for extended periods of time.
2) Have Patti and others move throughout the classroom in novel ways (e.g., walking backwards/sideways, hopping, crawling, etc). Moving in this fashion allows gross motor development and stimulates muscle contractions in different muscle groups.
3) Proceed with the understanding that motor development results from gross to fine movement and from movement of the trunk to movement of the extremities.
4) Correlate physical education activities with classroom activities to provide reinforcement of academic concepts. (Example: The teacher can use a game entitled "Nifty Novelists" in a language arts lesson requiring basic locomotor skills as well as language skills. Patti will have the opportunity to develop greater levels of health-related fitness (muscle strength and endurance and cardio respiratory endurance) and writing skills. The equipment needed is 25-30 cones, 25-30 sheets of paper, pencils and music (preferably without lyrics). The playing area can be the gymnasium, lawn, blacktop area, or any other area that allows freedom of movement. Do the following:

Place the cones in a scattered formation around the playing area. Under each cone should be a piece of paper, with a brief statement that begins a story, and a pencil. When the music starts students perform designated movements (hopping, skipping, etc.) around the area touching as many cones as possible. When the music stops, each student lifts the nearest cone and constructs another line to the story. This is repeated until a creative story is developed. Students are encouraged to write complete thoughts, including proper grammar (depending on the grade level).
5) Allow Patti to work at her desk/table in any position that is comfortable for her.

The specialists made the following specific suggestions:

1. Have Patti erase/wash the chalkboards daily.
2. Have Patti manipulate clay prior to a writing activity.
3. Have Patti cut out objects out of clay, straws, sandpaper, oak tag, felt, leather, to build hand strength.
4. Read stories aloud and ask the children to describe and act out what a certain person in the story did. Patti will have the ability to become "physical" with her creativity.
5. Throughout the day, provide opportunities for Patti to lift, carry, and move objects within the classroom as well as throughout her school. (e.g., carrying books back to the library, carrying recess equipment back into the building, etc.).
6. Suggest to the family to provide numerous lifetime and leisure activities for Patti at home (e.g., swimming, bike riding, walking, jumping rope, etc.).

The specialists recommended reviewing Patti's program in six to eight weeks. The teacher noted that after engaging in these activities and communicating with the family that Patti is engaging in a wide variety of physical activities. Progress is slow; however, the teacher has observed that Patti is not as tired as before, especially in the afternoons, and appears to show signs of more energy as she participates in classroom activities. The physical education teacher made an additional suggestion: to have Patti become a "helper" in the Kindergarten P.E. classes. Here she will have the opportunity to "demonstrate" numerous activities, participate physically in more structured settings, and more importantly improve her self-esteem.

Basic Sensory Function

If One or More of These Characteristics Are Exhibited . . .

- ❏ Pushes, shoves, kicks when standing in line or crowds
- ❏ Dislikes being touched
- ❏ Prefers touching rather then being touched
- ❏ Difficulty identifying objects by touch alone
- ❏ Excessive mouthing of objects
- ❏ Cannot find body parts with eyes closed
- ❏ Fearful of movement (going up and down stairs)
- ❏ Never gets dizzy (craves spinning and rolling)
- ❏ Gets dizzy easily (avoids spinning and rolling)
- ❏ Routinely smells nonfood objects
- ❏ Seeks out certain tastes or smells
- ❏ Becomes anxious or distressed when feet leave the ground
- ❏ Fears falling
- ❏ Dislikes head being upside down
- ❏ Avoids climbing and jumping
- ❏ Seeks all kinds of movement and this interferes with daily life
- ❏ Avoids playground equipment or moving toys
- ❏ Rocks body without realizing it
- ❏ Takes excessive risks while playing, has no safety awareness
- ❏ Twirls or spins self frequently during the day

Try These Activities

(Some activities incorporate more than one sensory skill and are listed under the appropriate categories.)

Vestibular

_____ Have the child sit on T-stool or therapy ball. (Also Equilibrium, Proprioceptive/Kinesthetic)

_____ The child sits on a large truck or tractor inner tube and bounces repeatedly on it.

_____ Lying prone on a scooter board, the child spins self around and around.

_____ Have the child stand on a rocker board.

_____ Have child stand on rocker board.

Tactile

_____ Have the tactile-defensive child stand in the back of a line of children so she will not have to negotiate space around herself.

_____ Squeeze/pinch clay prior to writing activity.

_____ Draw letters in flattened clay with a pencil or chopsticks.

_____ Allow the child to choose alternate positions for working; e.g., on stomach on floor, curled up in corner, etc.

_____ Suggest that the child wear tight-fitting clothing; e.g., tights, spandex, suspenders or weighted vest.

_____ Have the child sit on his hands.

_____ Provide a tactile bin in the classroom for "down time."

_____ Trace sandpaper letters with index finger.

_____ Trace letters on carpet samples with index finger.

_____ Have the child form letters with chenille stems or clay.

_____ Whenever touching the child, make sure that your touch is deep and firm.

_____ Allow the child to play barefoot. Receptors on the soles of the feet signal changes in texture and weight.

_____ To improve tactile awareness, provide opportunities for the child to feel and manipulate various materials; e.g., aerosal foam, shaving cream, whipping cream, pudding, hand lotion, and finger paints.

_____ To improve tactile discrimination try:

        Finger games/songs.

        Play a game to guess what you feel (discriminate textures, shapes, and objects).

        Try crawling or rolling on textures without looking and then guess what the materials are.

_____ Have the child suck thickened foods such as pudding, yogurt, and fruit-flavored gelatin, through a straw. Start with a short straw and progress to longer and longer straws.

Motor Planning

_____ Have the children do "mystery writing" at chalkboard with their eyes closed. Guide their hands to write letters or words and then have them guess what they wrote.

_____ Have the child draw letters in flattened clay with chopstick.

_____ Have the child trace various sizes of templates or cutouts at the chalkboard/whiteboard. (Also Tactile)

_____ Play the game "Do as I Do." Child names body parts as they as are touched with both hands.

_____ Practice slow motion jumping jacks. Work on arm movement, then movement of feet, and finally combine the two actions.

Bilateral Motor Coordination

_____ Squeeze/pinch clay prior to writing activity; alternate hands.

Proprioceptive/Kinesthetic

_____ Have student sit facing a partner, holding hands and feet in contact with legs extended. One student leans forward and the other student leans back, then reverse roles for rowboat action.

_____ Practice making circles with arms while holding dumbbells.

_____ Two children stand facing each other in forward stride position, right feet placed side by side, and right hands grasped. On signal "Go," each tries to push or pull the other to make him move his feet or lose balance.

_____ Have the child assist with moving classroom furniture. Try smaller items first and progress to larger and heavier ones, as the child seems able. (Also Tactile)

_____ Suggest that child wear tight-fitting clothing; e.g., tights, spandex, suspenders, or weighted vest.

_____ Have the child sit on hands. (Also Tactile)

_____ Place sandbags, beanbags, or bolsters on child's lap.

_____ Incorporate deep pressure exercises into daily routine:
  ► shifting weight in sitting from side to side
  ► pressing hands together
  ► putting hands on top of head and pressing down
  ► crossing arms and press on shoulders with opposite hands
  ► putting hands on knees and pressing down

> ▶ putting hands under opposite elbows and press up
> ▶ rotating shoulders and then upper trunk side to side
> ▶ tilting head rhythmically side to side
> ▶ brushing hands down arms firmly

_____ Use maximum stimuli such as the following in teaching new skills:

> ▶ Kinesthetic stimuli: guide the child's body parts through desired movement for a physical sense of the pattern.
> ▶ Tactile stimuli: use touch to relate more effectively to the child which part of the body is to be used; also, the child may learn more about the equipment and environment by touch.
> ▶ Visual stimuli: use visual aids such as slides, diagrams, demonstrations, pictures, films, and mirrors. Be aware that mirrors may confuse understanding of right and left concepts.
> ▶ Verbal stimuli: give oral instructions as the child performs.

_____ Let students put their hands on your shoulders or hips or be led physically so they receive the kinesthetic feeling of the following concepts:

> ▶ Time—show fast, slow, or uneven time by running or walking with the students.
> ▶ Space—lead the students around so they understand distances and the area of the classroom.
> ▶ Size—physically show the students how to be tall, short, or wide, and relate this to their environment.

_____ Allow the child to play barefoot. Receptors on the soles of the feet signal changes in texture and weight.

_____ Have the children move their heads, shoulders, arms, hands, or trunks while sitting or lying. (Also Motor Planning)

_____ Have students push and pull using elbows, arms, hands, and trunks while lying, sitting, or standing. (Also Motor Planning)

_____ Encourage the children to bend, stretch, twist, turn, and shake as many parts of their bodies as possible while standing, sitting, or lying. (Also Motor Planning)

Equilibrium

_____ With arms folded across the chest, the child squats. Keeping the knees bent, she jumps forward several times.

_____ Allow the child to blow bubbles with bubble solution and then break them by clapping hands together or touching them with elbow, thumb, or nose.

_____ Squeeze small balloons filled with flour.

_____ Hide objects in rice, sand, or styrene foam packing material in the tactile bin. Have the child dig in the bin to find the objects.

_____ Have the child sit in chair backwards so that the legs straddle the seat and the chest is against the back of the chair.

_____ Proceed with motor development from gross to fine movements and from movement of the trunk to movement of the extremities.

_____ Have the children move in different directions and in various ways to develop dynamic and static balance.

General Suggestions

_____ Student can have a desk in his "own space."

_____ When sitting with the group, have student sit in a corner seat.

_____ Create classroom environment that calms down or peps up the child (as appropriate).

_____ Allow children enough room to have some freedom of movement but make the area confining enough to maintain order and interest in the activity.

_____ Encourage children to work and move in space to be aware of their relationship to others and their environment.

_____ Provide the child with experiences in manipulating his environment.

_____ Use resistive activities. For example, pull back on the student's arm as he tries to bring it forward.

_____ Use a variety of auditory, tactile, visual, and proprioceptive modalities in isolation and in combination to teach activities.

_____ Use activities in which the child must identify her body parts, move them, and be aware of their positions in space.

_____ Provide activities to improve spatial awareness, laterality, directionality, body image, skillful movement performances, postural maintenance, and locating of sounds or objects.

_____ Emphasize activities that develop awareness of sensory input of touch, smell, taste, hearing, and proprioception.

_____ Provide kinesthetic cues, which may range from a signal, such as a tap on the shoulder, to actually leading the child through the movement.

VISUAL PERCEPTUAL PROBLEMS

If One or More of These Characteristics Are Exhibited . . .

- ❑ Has a diagnosed visual defect
- ❑ Poor understanding of spatial concepts (large, small, and numerical)
- ❑ Poor directional concepts (up, down, right, left, in, out)
- ❑ Difficulty putting puzzles together
- ❑ Difficulty recognizing shapes and colors
- ❑ Difficulty identifying object from the background
- ❑ Poor spacing on work paper
- ❑ Reverses letters, numbers, words, or phrases
- ❑ Difficulty with eye tracking
- ❑ Is bothered by bright lights

Try These Activities

(Some activities incorporate more than one sensory/motor skill and are listed under the appropriate categories.)

Tactile

_____ Trace sandpaper letters with index finger.

_____ Have the child form letters with chenille stems or clay.

_____ Encourage the child to pop soap bubbles or plastic bubble wrap with one finger or between two hands.

_____ Have the child do various map tracings which involve choosing a destination and planning a trip. Encourage him to find the longest route, the shortest route, the straightest, the curviest, etc.

_____ Chose a shape and have the child find objects in the room that are the same shape and bring them to you.

_____ Have the child play various memory games involving objects, such as "What's Missing?"

Vestibular

_____ Walk backward on a line towards a target.

_____ Provide the child with a variety of opportunities to spin in clockwise and counterclockwise motions, such as on a tire swing, a scooter board, an office chair that rotates, around a pole while holding on with one hand, etc. This helps to strengthen the muscles used for visual tracking.

_____ Have the child jump over a rope while it moves back and forth, or wiggles like a snake. Once the children have mastered this activity, see if they can clap their hands while jumping over the rope to increase the amount of sequencing required as they watch the rope. (Also Equilibrium)

_____ Create a large, multiple-step obstacle course with various stations to go through. Give the child a map of the route to follow through the course. Change the route each time she goes through the obstacle course and give her a new map to follow.

Motor Planning

_____ Complete puzzles that have small interlocking pieces.

_____ Draw lines to complete dot-to-dot pictures.

_____ The child retrieves something in the room but first must explain where the item is located without pointing.

_____ Encourage the child to "catch" a beam of light from a flashlight with both hands. Also have her jump on the beam with both feet.

_____ Use a super-bounce ball to play catch with the student. (Also Bilateral Motor Coordination)

_____ Have the child reorganize pictures cut into parts; e.g., a face cut into three parts, a bottle or ball cut in half, or an animal cut in half.

_____ Encourage the child to draw pictures to illustrate a story.

Bilateral Motor Coordination

_____ Make simultaneous vertical, horizontal or diagonal lines on the chalkboard, going in both directions. Also have the child try to write with both hands going in opposite directions.

_____ Try to pop soap bubbles with one finger or between two hands.

_____ Hit a suspended ball with a dowel using two hands.

_____ Place a table tennis ball inside a ring-shaped gelatin mold. Tilt the mold so that the ball rolls rhythmically around inside it.

_____ Have a balloon suspended from a string which is held at ends by two students. Two other students bat the balloon back and forth across the string with right hand, and then with left hand.

_____ Allow the child to bounce and catch a large rubber ball using both hands. Change the size of the ball for variation.

_____ Child tries to toss a ball into a basket from a position outside of a circle.

_____ Children pass and receive different-sized balls, moving them as rapidly as possible while standing in a circle.

_____ Draw a simple form or pattern on the whiteboard while the child watches you. Erase the image quickly and thoroughly. Have the child redraw it.

Proprioceptive/Kinesthetic

_____ While the child holds a dowel upright in both hands, have him catch rings tossed to him.

Equilibrium

____ Have the child walk backward on a line towards a target behind you.

____ Provide the child with a variety of opportunities to spin around in both clockwise and counterclockwise directions, such as on a tire swing, a scooter board, an office chair that rotates, around a pole while holding on with one hand, etc. This helps to strengthen the muscles used for visual tracking. (Also Proprioceptive/Kinesthetic)

General Considerations

____ Use a multisensory approach to teaching.

____ Determine if there is also a tactile problem.

____ Encourage the student to make a space two fingers in width between each word when writing sentences.

____ Highlight margins on paper.

____ Color-code papers for student—green for top, yellow for middle, red for bottom.

____ Play gross motor games involving spatial awareness skills.

____ At appropriate times, brainstorm solutions with the child to develop problem-solving skills.

____ Work with the child to divide the process into smaller steps.

____ Have the child reproduce from memory a horizontal array of pictures, objects, letters, numbers, etc.

Social and Emotional Problems

If One or More of These Characteristics Are Exhibited . . .

- ❏ Verbally aggressive
- ❏ Bothers others
- ❏ Happiest playing alone, isolates self from others
- ❏ Physically aggressive
- ❏ Attention seeking
- ❏ Impulsive
- ❏ Lacks confidence
- ❏ Cries easily
- ❏ Fearful of new situations
- ❏ Easily frustrated
- ❏ Falls asleep in class
- ❏ Cannot calm down
- ❏ Has difficulty making friends
- ❏ Is overly serious
- ❏ Does not express emotions

General Considerations

_____ Have information available on the nature of the difficulty, including past histories and other pertinent data.

_____ Keep records of performance and information concerning the student's conduct.

_____ Invite the student several times to join an activity with others but do not force her to participate.

_____ Do not be surprised by a student's disruptive behavior. If the student gains very little by his unruliness, these episodes may become less frequent and eventually lead him to a more acceptable manner of dealing with his emotions.

_____ Teach the student new skills so that she gains a sense of achievement.

_____ Teach students how to relax using yoga techniques, music, rhythms, etc.

_____ For tense individuals, include mild rhythmic exercises during the school day.

_____ Provide the majority of the instruction on a one-to-one basis or in a small group.

_____ Provide immediate reinforcement for desired behavior; awarding ribbons or certificates stimulates participation.

_____ Read facial expressions and body gestures to anticipate the future actions of then student.

_____ Set up the class according to a routine or orderly procedure. If students know what is coming next, they are more secure.

_____ Have a prompt and consistent approach to starting work.

_____ Help students remember better by using visual aids.

_____ Make students feel secure; experiences must not be threatening.

_____ Increase the attention span of students by removing distracting objects.

_____ Do not strive for control at all times. Allow free-play periods.

_____ Follow programs that stress the development of social competency and personal adequacy.

_____ Use the following intervention methods to control behavior:

- ► Planned ignoring
- ► Interest boosting: if a child's interest is waning, involve him actively in the class activity at that moment and let him demonstrate the skill that is being performed or discussed.
- ► Reduction of tension through humor
- ► Planned success: sometimes a child is frustrated by a task she is requested to perform. Instead of asking for help, she may involve her peers in disruptive activity. In this event, structure a task in which the child can be successful.
- ► Restructuring of the program
- ► Positive and negative reinforcement

_____ Teach the child how to play and enjoy activity.

_____ Prevent students from experiencing embarrassment and failure while their behavior is still unstable.

_____ Include activities in the program that the child has had experience completing.

_____ Group participation in activities is desirable because of the social contacts it makes necessary.

_____ Provide opportunities for free play rather than structure the entire school day.

_____ Praise movements that are performed well. It will help to build a good self-concept.

_____ Vary activities because students have short attention spans.

_____ Let students express inner feelings.

_____ Use drama to describe everyday happenings.

_____ Help students to handle various situations they may encounter in their lives.

_____ Help students feel comfortable in a variety of dramatized situations.

_____ Let students express their feelings in an acceptable way.

_____ Help students learn how to work in a group.

_____ Use story plays to allow students to express their feeling of fear, hatred, or frustration.

_____ Share familiar stories that may be of more interest to students.

_____ Use story plays as a tool for encouraging a child to practice listening skills.

_____ Read poetry aloud to children, stopping frequently to allow them to finish the phrases with rhyming words

_____ Provide ample opportunities for children to express themselves in creative drama and to demonstrate their perception of the environment around them.

Case Study

David is a sixth grader attending middle school. He changes classes and often has difficulty interacting with his peers. His middle school teachers have filled out the Pre-Referral Motor Screening Checklist and note that David is often verbally aggressive, physically aggressive, impulsive, easily frustrated, and has difficulty making friends. Due to these characteristics displayed daily, David has had great difficulty staying on task during class activities. Homework is also a problem, as he often does not complete the work. His counselor, school psychologist, and adapted physical education (A.P.E.) specialist were called in to observe. Each issue noted by his teachers was confirmed in the observations made. The specialists made the following general recommendations for his teachers:

1) Collect information available on the nature of the difficulty, including past histories and other pertinent data. Meet with and interview David's parents for further and present information.
2) Keep clear and concise records of episodes and other information concerning David's interactions with his peers.
3) Provide immediate reinforcement for desired behavior.
4) All of David's teachers need to be consistent in their approach to planning lessons and dealing with undesirable behavior.
5) Do not strive for control at all times—allow David to have short periods of "down time" if necessary.
6) Provide group activities facilitating social contact when appropriate.
7) Praise David's accomplishments in class that are performed well; it will help to build his self-esteem.

The specialists also made specific suggestions of ideas that can be implemented for David to participate in:

1) If necessary, provide the majority of David's instruction one-on-one or in a small group and gradually increase the contact time in the large-class activity.
2) Provide opportunities throughout the day for David to express his inner feelings.
3) Provide activities that will ensure success for David.
4) Use familiar stories or interests that may stimulate David's interest in curriculum offerings.
5) "Teach" David how to enjoy activities and interact with this joy.
6) Use creative drama to allow David to express himself.
7) Often David's episodes cause embarrassment and failure for him. His

teachers need to be aware of this fact and protect him while this behavior is still unstable.

8) Meet biweekly with all teachers and specialists to discuss progress. If progress is noted, these meetings can gradually become monthly.

9) Provide opportunities for physically appropriate outlets for David throughout the day (e.g., going to the gym and shooting baskets, jogging or walking around the building with a peer, using fitness equipment if available, etc.).

This program needed to be coordinated carefully due to the nature of the middle school. David has four primary teachers on his team and numerous specialists in the building. All teachers needed to be consistent in their approach. By adhering to the biweekly meetings, David's teachers were able to produce a program for him that was nurturing, consistent in delivery of instruction, and consistent in the handling of undesirable episodes. Some strategies the team came up with were: planned ignoring when necessary, reducing tension through humor, restructuring the program as necessary, and using music for relaxation opportunities. The school psychologist maintained leadership throughout this process. Physical activities were provided by the physical education staff and it was suggested to the team that David could participate in another section of P.E. for his favorite sport—basketball—as an appropriate outlet. Physical activity has shown to improve health-related fitness and can enhance self-esteem. David's progress has been steady and he has made improvements in his ability to interact with others in a positive way.

Bilateral Integration Problems

If One or More of These Characteristics Are Exhibited . . .

- ❏ Avoids or has difficulty performing tasks which require eyes or extremities to cross the midline
- ❏ Neglects or seems unaware of one side
- ❏ Does not stabilize paper while writing
- ❏ Seems to ignore one half of page
- ❏ Has an inconsistent hand dominance
- ❏ Always uses both hands together
- ❏ Nondominant hand remains inactive (does not stabilize paper)
- ❏ Confuses or reverses letters and numerals
- ❏ Avoids diagonal strokes
- ❏ Demonstrates overflow movements (one hand unconsciously mirrors what the other hand is doing with no purposeful reason)

Try These Activities

(Some activities incorporate more than one sensory/motor skill and are listed under the appropriate categories.)

Vestibular

_____ Have a child jump a short rope, using various movements.

_____ While standing in place, the child jumps with both feet forward, sideways, and backward. Arms should swing at sides of body.

Tactile

_____ Encourage the child to pop soap bubbles or plastic bubble wrap with one finger, with one hand, or between two hands.

_____ Use kinesthetic and tactile activities to reinforce letter formation as the student writes and traces his commonly reversed letters and numbers on the blackboard, fine sandpaper, or play clay.

Motor Planning

_____ Have the child trace various sizes of templates or cutouts at the chalkboard/whiteboard. (Also Tactile)

_____ Play the game "Do as I Do." Child names body parts as they are touched with both hands.

_____ Practice slow motion jumping jacks. Work on arm movement, then movement of feet, and finally combine the two actions.

Bilateral Motor Coordination

____ Encourage the child to use a stapler and hole puncher on sheets of scrap paper. (Also Tactile, Proprioceptive/Kinesthetic)

____ Have student raise arms out to the side and make large and small circles, forward and backward with fast and slow motions.

____ The child rolls a ball around a hoop placed on the floor, controlling the ball with her feet.

____ Have the student roll the ball around a hoop with his hands while crawling on knees.

Proprioceptive/Kinesthetic

____ Have the child assist with moving classroom furniture. Try smaller items first and then progress to larger and heavier ones, as child seems able. (Also Tactile)

____ Have the child make circles with arms while holding dumbbells.

____ Have the child secure papers together using spring-loaded paper clips. (Also Tactile, Bilateral Motor Coordination)

____ Incorporate "wake up" activities such as jumping jacks and other calisthenics or a fast-paced game of "Simon Says" involving finger, thumb, and hand and arm movements. (Also Vestibular)

General Suggestions

____ Assure proper chair and desk height.

____ Encourage cursive writing. It sometimes eliminates letter reversals.

____ Use directional cues paired with verbal ones; e.g., "d" faces the diamond drawn on the upper-left corner of the page and "b" and "p" face the pink ball on the upper-right corner.

____ Use other techniques for correcting reversals:
  - Show how lowercase "b" is like the capital "B" without the top circle.
  - Remember pictures such as bed (bed), bat, and ball.
    To remember "d": make a "c" first; add a line to make "d"
  - With palms facing the chest and thumbs up, the student makes two fists; the left hand will form a "b" and the right hand will form a "d."
  - Develop an individual cue card for each student to keep at her desk with common reversals

____ Have child work on a vertical surface; with this orientation, "up" and "down" refer literally to hand movements the student performs.

Educators—What You Can Do

1. Read! Get your hands on information about sensory integration dysfunction. Take time to familiarize yourself with its characteristics, behaviors, general information, and current literature concerning this dysfunction.

2. Attend workshops, in-service training, and conferences to increase your working knowledge of sensory integration. Experts and persons who have extensive experience and knowledge concerning educating children with SI dysfunction have much to share.

3. Work with your educational colleagues, not in isolation. Do not take it upon yourself to educate the children alone. Their needs are many and the spectrums of stimuli they need should be addressed interactively with all persons working with these children.

4. Work with your administrator and special education support personnel to continue to strive for the needs of the child in the educational setting. If there are barriers present that may hinder or slow the educational process, than you need the support and cooperation of the administration to remove all barriers that impeded the child's education.

5. Work closely with parents to develop a program that is "workable" for the child. Educators and parents should be in harmony and in support of each other as they both strive for the best education for the child. Parents need to express their wants and teachers need to express their observations so that the two schools of thought can be analyzed and educational plans made accordingly for the child. Parents should not dictate and teachers should not resist new ideas or we would be working with a negative rather than a positive model.

6. Be honest and forthright. When you are unsure or do not always possess the knowledge to deal with an issue—it is okay to seek additional information to help the child succeed in learning.

7. Be direct and professional when you are providing information at meetings and/or parent conferences. Tell it like it is. Do not "sugar coat" the issue when you know professionally that it is otherwise. What you say at a meeting can affect a child's education for months or longer.

8. Analyze reading materials. Make sure you know who the authors are and in what context the articles have been written. Some experts or researchers in their settings may evaluate children and draw conclusions concerning their behaviors and potential to learn. A

speech pathologist, physical therapist, and occupational therapist may see children with special needs in a clinical setting one or two times or more per week in a one-to-one or small therapy group. However, educators see the child in an educational setting in an inclusive classroom with other children with special needs. For the inclusive child in a classroom with at least 20 other students, it is a very different setting. The specialists may come up with criteria, goals, and objectives that may indicate the present level of functioning for these children. However, these evaluations may not be true indicator of their performance levels in a school setting.

9. Do not avoid positive conflict. It is okay to disagree with parents and colleagues about the strategies or techniques that you are using with the child as long as you and the others can resolve the issue in a positive manner that ultimately benefits the child.

10. Collect information on the child's background, particularly the most recent months of his life. What type of environment at home does he have? What experiences has he had? What types of stimuli does he bring to the program? What motivates the child?

11. Time is an important concept. Children with sensory integration dysfunction need significant amounts of time to learn. They need time to process sensory information presented to them. They may need repetitive opportunities in classroom activities. They will also need continuity throughout the learning process. Good things will come out if you use this concept properly. Frustration and discouragement can occur in time if it is not used properly. Keeping the concept of time in mind, you will become much more student-orientated, rather then curriculum-based. Children with sensory integration dysfunction develop at their rates. They seldom perform to the schedules of either educators or anxious parents.

Glossary of Terms

Sensory Integration Terms

adaptive response • a suitable achievement in which the child responds effectively to environmental demands; the processing of sensory information takes place; furthers the sensory integrative process

body image • a child's feelings concerning his body; the sensory images or "maps" of the body stored in the brain; also called body scheme

brain stem • the lowest portion of the brain; connects the spinal chord with the cerebrum; controls vital organs; perceives sensory information and handles elementary sensory-motor processing

co-contraction • the synchronized contraction of all muscles around a joint to stabilize it

dyspraxia • poor coordination displayed by some children, sometimes evident in handwriting and eye-hand coordination; often related to poor somatosensory processing

extension • the movement of body parts that straighten out at the joints (neck, back, arms, and legs)

flexion • the movement of body parts that bend at the joints (neck, back, arms, and legs)

gravitational insecurity • a child's apprehension related to head position; causes feelings of anxiety or fear; usually related to unclear messages from the vestibular and proprioception systems

hypersensitivity to movement • disorientation from vigorous activity in the form of headaches, nausea, or dizziness; may occur up to several hours after receiving the input

kinesthesia • perception of the body in space from received sensory information through the joints, muscles, and tendons

lateralization • is the localization of the control center in the brain for a particular function to be processed on one side of the brain. In most people, the right hemisphere becomes more efficient in processing spatial information, while the left hemisphere of the brain specializes in verbal and logical processes.

learning disorder • a difficulty in learning to read, write, or compute that cannot be attributed to impaired sight or hearing, or to mental retardation

0-7424-0268-1 • Sensory Integratio

modulation • the brain's regulation of its own activity; involves facilitating some neural messages to maximize a response and blocking other messages to reduce irrelevant activity

nystagmus • a series of automatic, back-and-forth eye movements indicating impaired muscle function of the eye; reflex produced by different conditions

occupational therapy • is a health-care profession concerned with improving a person's occupational performance. In a pediatric setting, the therapist evaluates a child's performance in relation to what is developmentally expected for that age group. If there is a discrepancy between functional ability and developmental expectations, the therapist looks at a variety of perceptual and neuromuscular factors that influence function. Based on knowledge of neurology, kinesiology, development, medical diagnoses, and current research, the therapist can identify children who have the best potential for remediation through this type of therapy.

perception • the child's ability to process sensory information about the environment or incoming stimuli

physical therapy • is a health-care profession concerned with improving a person's physical ability. In a pediatric setting, the physical therapist evaluates a child's orthopedic structure and neuromuscular functions. A physical therapist can also receive special training identical to that received by an occupational therapist to assess and remediate the disorders in sensory processing that influence learning and behavior.

praxis (motor planning) • the child's ability to engage in activities in a sequential manner; able to complete a sequence of unfamiliar actions

prone • the child lying face down on surface

proprioception • perception of sensory nerve endings in muscles, tendons, and joints that provides a sense of the body's position in space by responding to incoming stimuli; refers to sensations from the muscles and joints; indicates where each part of the body is and how it is moving

sensory input • incoming stimuli from the senses to the brain and spinal cord

sensory integration • the organization of sensory input for use; the "use" may be a perception of the body or the world, an adaptive response, a learning process, or the development of some neural function. Through sensory integration, the many parts of the nervous system work together so that a person can interact with the environment effectively and experience appropriate satisfaction

sensory integrative dysfunction • is an irregularity or disorder in brain function that makes it difficult to integrate sensory input effectively. Sensory integrative dysfunction may be present in motor, learning, social/emotional, speech/language, or attention disorders.

somatosensory • body sensations that are based on both tactile and proprioceptive information

specialization • the process in which one side of the brain more readily adapts than the other side to particular functions or conditions in response to environmental factors

supine • the child lying on back with face upward

tactile • relating to the sense of touch on the skin

tactile defensiveness • a sensory integrative dysfunction in which tactile sensations create negative emotional reactions; associated with distractibility, restlessness, and behavior problems

vestibular system • the sensory system that responds to the position of the head in relation to gravity and accelerated or decelerated movement; integrates neck, eye, and body adjustments to movement

Motor Terms

The following terms can assist the teacher in the development of a "motor vocabulary."

active listening • the child listens with awareness of both verbal and nonverbal communication of others

adaptive behavior • the result the child displays as she processes social, physical, and mental demands of the environment

adaptive skills • having integrated specific sensory information, the child learns patterns of behavior to meet his needs and the needs of others.

agility • the child displays a combination of speed, suppleness, and skill

agnosia • the inability to recognize familiar people or objects, usually caused by brain dysfunction

agonist • a muscle whose action is balanced by that of another connected muscle

akinesia • the loss or lessening of the normal power of movement

antagonist • a muscle that operates with and limits the action of another muscle

aphasia • a partial or total inability to produce and understand speech as a result of brain dysfunction

apraxia • inability to perform complex movements

association • the organized process of relating the sensory information with the motor act; relating past and present motor experiences with each other

ataxia • the inability to coordinate the movements of muscles

athetotic movement • writhing, irregular, arrhythmic gross movement

balance • the state in which a body or object remains reasonably steady against the force of gravity

body awareness • understanding of how the body parts move

body image • perception of the body as derived from motor experiences

body scheme • the ability to use skeletal and muscle functions to make adjustments in movement

cardio-respiratory endurance • the ability of the heart and lungs to maintain efficient function during and after vigorous activity

cerebral dominance • one side of the brain is more developed than the other (for example, right-handedness is controlled by the left hemisphere of the brain)

contracture • a permanent muscular contraction

coordination • the harmonious working together of several muscles or muscle groups in the execution of complicated motor movements

developmental delay • a lag of maturation in one of the motor, cognitive, or emotional states

directionality • the child's ability to perceive space outside of the body within the environment

dynamic balance • the ability to maintain a position while the individual is moving or the surface is moving

dyspraxia • difficulty in completing a motor act

equilibrium • a physical state; the sense of being able to maintain the body in balance

eye-foot coordination • the ability to use eyes and feet together to complete a task

eye-hand coordination • the ability to use eyes and hands together to complete a task

figure-ground discrimination • the ability to distinguish objects from their backgrounds

fine motor coordination • the ability of muscles to perform small movements

flexibility • the ability of the body part to move through its entire range of motion

gross motor coordination • the child's ability to move the total body through space efficiently and smoothly

haptic sense • the combination of the sense of touch and kinesthetic information

hemiparesis • muscular weakness of one side of the body

hemiplegia • the total or partial inability to move one side of the body

hyperesthesia • the increased sensitivity to touch

hypertonia • greater than normal muscle tension

hypotonia • less than normal muscle tension

ipsilateral • occurring or affecting one side of the body

locomotor movements • movements performed while moving the body from place to place, e.g., skipping, hopping, running, walking

manipulative skills • combinations of fine and gross motor skills, usually involving the hands

modeling • the demonstration of an action; example for imitation

monoplegia • the paralysis of one limb

motor planning • the ability to move, plan, and execute a group of movement skills

motor skills • a specific set of movement responses requiring correctness and accuracy

motor task • a specific movement skill or pattern; may be directed by therapist for performance by the student

movement education • a physical education approach utilizing basic movement patterns

movement exploration • teaching physical education curriculum through nondirective methods in which the child explores the environment using basic movement patterns

movement flow • movement that is efficiently sequenced and smooth

muscular endurance • the capacity of the muscles to maintain activity requiring muscular strength without undue fatigue

neuron • a specialized cell in the nervous system

ocular regressions • a right-to-left movement of the eye made in a reverse direction while individual reads

paralysis • the loss of voluntary movement as a result of damage to nerve or muscle function

paraparesis • a partial paralysis or weakness in lower extremities

paraplegia • the paralysis of muscles in lower extremities

perception • the process of using the senses to obtain information about the adjacent environment and circumstances

proprioception • the sense of balance, position in space, and changes in equilibrium of a body part during motor movements by receiving stimulus from muscles, tendons, and joints

quadriparesis • partial paralysis or weakness in all four extremities

quadriplegia • the paralysis of muscles in all four extremities

reflex • responses which occur automatically and involuntarily as a result of the nervous system's reaction to a stimulus

righting reactions • the body's ability to bring itself into its normal position in space; sensory information flows from labyrinth, eyes, muscles, and skin

rigidity • a body part not bending or moving easily through the range of motion, due to inflexible and tonic contraction of muscles

self-image • how an individual perceives himself or herself as a person; feelings of worth, appearance, and intelligence

sensory-motor • integrating the senses and movement responses

spastic • characterized by spasms and resulting in hypertonia and awkward movements from stiff muscles

spasticity • a state of hypertonicity; increased muscle tone

spatial relations • the relationship of the skeletal parts of the body to each other and to objects in the environment

static balance • balance in which the support is stable and the individual is not in locomotion

stereognosis • the ability to recognize solid objects by their touch

tactile defensiveness • the child's inability to tolerate certain types of touch; resistive and uncomfortable with certain kinds of touch (believed to be form of sensory integrative dysfunction)

underreactive • responding minimally or slowly to stimuli

Terms Linking Motor and Academics

arm strength • the child's ability to demonstrate muscular contractions and endurance of the arms for a period of time

audio-motor • the ability to process auditory information and respond by completing a motor task

abdominal strength • the child's ability to demonstrate muscular contractions and endurance of the abdominal muscles; the ability of the abdominal muscles to support internal organs and lower back

balance-postural orientation • the child's ability to hold her body in static and dynamic positions

color discrimination • the ability to distinguish different colors and tints

endurance • the child's ability to maintain vigorous activity over relatively long periods of time

explosive leg power • the child's ability to demonstrate muscular contractions and endurance of the lower extremities

eye-hand coordination • the child's ability to use the eyes to direct one's hands in motor tasks

eye-hand accuracy • the ability to use the eyes and hands efficiently in precise movements requiring the eyes and hands to work together

eye-foot accuracy • the child's ability to coordinate the eye and foot in motor tasks

form discrimination • the child's ability to distinguish between objects that vary in shape or form

gross body coordination • the child's ability to move her body efficiently when performing a motor task

kinesthetic-motor • the child's ability to process information through the joints and maintain an appropriate position in space

serialization • the ability to perform a series of motor tasks in a sequence consistent with the directions provided

tactile-motor • the child's ability to process tactile information and respond motorically

visual-motor response • the child's ability to process visual information and respond motorically

Bibliography

Abraham, Michael C. *Adapted Phys Ed*. Grand Rapids, Michigan: McGraw-Hill Children's Publishing, 2000.

Abraham, Michael C. *Creative Rhythms and Movement*. Kearney, Nebraska: Educational Systems Associates, 2001.

Abraham, Michael C. *"Mommy . . . this is hard for me": A Perspective on the Student with Special Needs Who Is Included within the Regular Public School Classroom*. Kearney, Nebraska: Educational Systems Associates, 1998.

Armstrong Thomas. *ADD/ADHD Alternatives in the Classroom*. Alexandria, Virginia: Association for Supervision and Curriculum Development, 1999.

Arnheim, Daniel, and Sinclair, William. *The Clumsy Child*. St. Louis: C.V. Mosby Co. 1979.

Ayres, Jean. *Sensory Integration and the Child*. Los Angeles: Western Psychological Services, 1982.

Bishop, Paul. *Adapted Physical Education: A Comprehensive Resource Manual of Definition, Assessment, Programming, and Future Predictions*. Kearney, Nebraska: Educational Systems Associates, 1994.

Brehm, Madeleine, and Tindell, Nancy. *Movement with a Purpose: Perceptual Motor-Lesson Plans for Young Children*. West Nyack, N.Y.: Parker Publishing Company, 1983.

Capon, Jack. *Successful Movement Challenges*. Byron, California: Front Row Experience, 1981.

Geiger, Jo A. *AIM - Adventures in Movement*. Aim for the Handicapped Inc., 1979.

Gilroy, Pamela J. *Discovery in Motion – Movement Exploration for Problem-Solving and Self-Concept*. Tucson, Arizona: Communication Skill Builders, 1989.

Kamiya, Art. *Elementary Teacher's Handbook of Indoor and Outdoor Games*. West Nyack, NY: Parker Publishing Company, 1985.

New Games Foundation. *More New Games!* Garden City, N.Y.: Doubleday, 1981.

Schurr, Evelyn. *Movement Experiences for Children*. Englewoods Cliffs, N.J.: Prentice-Hall Inc., 1980.

Skinner, Louise. *Motor Development in the Preschool Years*. Springfield, Ill.: Charles C. Thomas, 1979.

Vodola, Thomas. *Diagnostic-Prescriptive Motor Ability and Physical Fitness Tasks and Activities*. Neptune City, N.J.: C.F. Wood Co., 1978.

Weikart, Phyllis, and Carlton, Elizabeth. *Foundations in Elementary Education*. Ypsilanti, Michigan: High/Scope Press, 1995.

Weikart, Phyllis. *Round the Circle*. Ypsilanti, Michigan: High/Scope Press, 1987.

Weikart, Phyllis. *Teaching Movement and Dance*. Ypsilanti, Michigan: High/Scope Press, 1989.